Oil Enough to Make the Journey

Oil Enough to Make the Journey

Sermons on the Christian Walk

JACK R. LUNDBOM
foreword by PHILIP A. AMERSON

CASCADE *Books* • Eugene, Oregon

OIL ENOUGH TO MAKE THE JOURNEY
Sermons on the Christian Walk

Copyright © 2022 Jack R. Lundbom. All rights reserved. Except for brief quotations in critical publications or reviews, no part of this book may be reproduced in any manner without prior written permission from the publisher. Write: Permissions, Wipf and Stock Publishers, 199 W. 8th Ave., Suite 3, Eugene, OR 97401.

Cascade Books
An Imprint of Wipf and Stock Publishers
199 W. 8th Ave., Suite 3
Eugene, OR 97401

www.wipfandstock.com

PAPERBACK ISBN: 978-1-667-0045-9
HARDCOVER ISBN: 978-1-667-0046-6
EBOOK ISBN: 978-1-667-0047-3

Cataloguing-in-Publication data:

Names: Lundbom, Jack R., author. | Amerson, Philip A., foreword.

Title: Oil enough to make the journey : sermons on the Christian walk / Jack R. Lundbom ; foreword by Philip A. Amerson.

Description: Eugene, OR: Cascade Books, 2022. | Includes index.

Identifiers: ISBN: 978-1-667-0045-9 (paperback). | ISBN: 978-1-667-0046-6 (hardcover). | ISBN: 978-1-667-0047-3 (ebook).

Subjects: LSCH: Evangelical Covenant Church of America—Sermons. | Christian life—Sermons. | Sermons, American.

Classification: BV4501.3 L8624 2022 (print). | BV4501.3 (ebook).

Scripture quotations throughout are from the RSV, NRSV, Anchor Bible (AB), or are my own.

Scripture quotations are taken from Jack R. Lundbom, *Jeremiah: A New Translation with Introduction and Commentary* (3 vols.; AB 21A–21C; New York: Doubleday, 1999–2004).

Scripture quotations are taken from Jack R. Lundbom, *Deuteronomy: A Commentary* (Grand Rapids: Eerdmans, 2013).

Scripture quotations are taken from the New Revised Standard Version Bible © 1989 National Council of the Churches of Christ in the United States of America. Used by permission. All rights reserved worldwide.

Scripture quotations marked (RSV) are taken from the Revised Standard Version of the Bible, copyright © 1946, 1952, and 1971 National Council of the Churches of Christ in the United States of America. Used by permission. All rights reserved worldwide.

Contents

Foreword by Philip A. Amerson | vii
Preface | xi
Introduction | xiii
Abbreviations | xvii

Walking with a Hidden and Revealed God

1. "I Will Be What I Will Be" | 3
2. The Injustice in Divine Grace | 9
3. "No Other Name" (Transfiguration) | 13
4. O Jerusalem, Jerusalem: You Spared Jeremiah—But Thanks Be to God! (Lent) | 19
5. Scriptures and Bread Broken Open (Easter) | 25
6. "A God Far Off" | 30
7. Something of Oneself, Something of Another (Christmas) | 35

Understanding the Christian Walk

8. The Sermon on the Mount | 41
9. "My Yoke Is Easy and My Burden Is Light" | 44
10. Invitation to Adventure (Lent) | 49
11. "What Is That to You? Follow Me" (Easter) | 55
12. Faith Seeks Understanding | 61
13. Christians Neither Hot Nor Cold (Worldwide Communion) | 65
14. Olive Shoots Around Your Table (Thanksgiving) | 69

Contents

Being Faithful in the Christian Walk

   15. What about Anger? | 77

   16. "To Obey Is Better Than Sacrifice" | 82

   17. Love Is Something You Do | 87

   18. The Indelicacy of Too-Ready Speech | 92

   19. "Peace, Peace, When There Is No Peace" | 96

   20. Sowing in Tears, Reaping with Shouts of Joy (Lent) | 99

   21. Mayonnaise, Mediators, and the Ministry of Barnabas | 104

   22. "When the Son of Man Comes, Will He Find Faith?" | 109

Stages of the Christian Walk

   23. The Challenge of Young Adulthood: Intimacy or Isolation? (Lent) | 117

   24. The Challenge of Midlife Transition: Creation or Destruction? (Lent) | 123

   25. The Challenge of Adulthood: Generativity or Stagnation? (Palm Sunday) | 128

   26. The Challenge of Mature Adulthood: Integrity or Despair? (Lent) | 134

   27. Reflecting the Glory | 140

   28. Old Christians but No Old Christianity | 146

   29. Old Soldiers Never Die | 151

Walking with Wisdom

   30. Oil Enough to Make the Journey (Advent) | 157

   31. The Limits of Wisdom | 161

   32. "A Time to Be Born and a Time to Die" (New Year's) | 167

Name Index | 173

Scripture Index | 175

Foreword

Markers along the Way

Philip A. Amerson

My best sermon ideas come while walking. Sometimes I walk alone, sometimes with a friend. I lumber along old familiar paths or trek off trail in a fresh, unmarked direction. Eventually, however, I return to the starting place and to the solitary task of sitting and writing. Preparation for me involves study, prayer, reading, writing, more reading, more prayer and, inevitably, rewriting. My sermons typically are preached after several walks. Other preachers, no doubt, have different approaches to sermon preparation, perhaps better.

Even when I am asked to preach an impromptu or extemporaneous sermon, I scan my memory bank to draw on some idea marinated earlier by studying and strolling. I will draw on something considered while ambling and noodling as part of the process.

Years ago I was privileged to know Dr. K. Morgan Edwards, renowned pastor and professor of preaching at First Methodist Church in Pasadena, California, and at the Claremont School of Theology. On occasion we would sit together and speak of homiletics. By the time I knew Morgan, he was wheelchair-bound and struggled with respiratory difficulties. His walking days were behind him, but not his thinking days. Our visits included my mining his wisdom and experience for insights about preachers and preaching. "It's a poorly kept secret," he would offer, "that good preachers read and ponder, and great preachers read a lot, and ponder even more." So, I felt some affirmation about my patterns of sermon preparation. Yet, still,

Foreword

I hoped my approach didn't lead to too many ponderous sermons! When I asked him how long it takes to prepare a great sermon, Morgan rose slightly in his wheelchair, struggled to catch his breath. Then, with dancing eyes, and in that sonorous baritone voice he announced, "A lifetime!"

In this collection, *Oil Enough to Make the Journey*, we are gifted with "walking sermons" from biblical scholar and theologian Jack Lundbom. These sermons are assembled from his work across a lifetime. These were preached from pulpits around the globe and are interwoven and interspersed with scholarship and pastoral work. They were proclaimed from the US to Zaire, from the United Kingdom to India, China, Norway, Lebanon and Australia—and back home again. One recognizes a sensitivity to cultural contexts and world events; these sermons are not dated, as their relevance shines through to our day. Over and again the word rings out that followers of Jesus join an ever-forward-moving adventure.

It would be a mistake to think of this collection as only for pastors or professional theologians. Here we find a "walking partner" who points us to the road ahead. Here we learn to say to those who question, "I WILL BE has sent me to you." It is the way of "an irrational God of grace." We are enriched in knowing Jeremiah as the great prophet of integrity and are given a fresh look at familiar parables along with lessons in "The Indelicacy of Too-Ready Speech." Here is the fruit of a comprehensible preacher who invites us to walk alongside. This collection spans the Christian liturgical year: from Christmas to Transfiguration, from Good Friday to Easter. Grace and judgement are found in each sermon, and grace prevails. It is the through line and dominant refrain. There is no diagnosis without pointing to a cure and no demand without offering the gift. Salvation, deliverance, and liberation are synonymous, or at least parallel keys, as the preacher invites us to make ready and join the journey.

My walking routes are more limited these days, hectored in by the COVID pandemic. Most often now I walk a trail through the forest a few miles south of my home. It is lesser known and a less populated trail than others I once took. The trail passes near quarries in this limestone rich region of Indiana. I note the large blocks of stone ready to be cut, designed and shipped for some building project far away.

Recently my eye caught something very different. There ahead of me was a strip of small stones and pieces of broken pottery all lined up on the edge of the path, unnoticed before. Some of these modest stones, larger than pebbles, have been painted a variety of colors. Some have elaborate

Foreword

designs, some are broken edges of china, some have words like *joy*, *faith*, *tears*, and *persist* painted on them. Others in this extended column of little rocks are plain, natural, smooth, or rugged. Carefully placed here by another, a stranger who journeys this path, or perhaps by a group of unknown walkers.

I now look forward to arriving at this memorial when I pass this way. It is now past thirty feet in length, more than one hundred items long. It appears this person, or these persons, are slowly and carefully making a record. To what? Or, to whom? I do not know. I do know this: The strip of stones and pottery shards grows longer as the months pass. Perhaps these mark some passage in a life. Perhaps someone is celebrating another month of sobriety. Or perhaps a journeyer near my age is honoring the passing of friends to death. Or perhaps another child has been born. In a sense it has become my memorial as well. I can attribute my own meanings to these stones.

In *Oil Enough to Make the Journey* we have much, much more than a line of small stones. These are not markers where we need to guess at the meanings. Here are markers that have been placed across the years that point to the dominant and overwhelming reality of the undeserved grace of God for us. Further, our walking need not be limited to one path in one locale. Rather, these sermons serve as markers scattered across time and geography. In my imaginings I can hear K. Morgan Edwards clearing his throat and in a sonorous baritone voice announcing, "These are markers of a lifetime of faith."

Philip A. Amerson
President Emeritus
Garrett-Evangelical Theological Seminary

Preface

Sermons in this book were preached in chapels of seminaries where I was teaching, in churches where I served as pastor, and in pulpits at home and abroad where I preached on invitation. The sermons span a period of years, and as a result speak to a variety of issues in our world, in America, in the church, and in the lives of people near and far. There was civil rights and social unrest over the Vietnam War in the 1960s; release of American hostages from Iran in 1981; the fortieth anniversary of the end of World War II, the fall of the Berlin Wall, and fall of Communism in Russia and Eastern Europe in the latter 1980s, and other events of greater or lesser magnitude that any preacher might feel under obligation to address. I have not expunged these references or sought to modify them, feeling that they can still speak to people today.

Currently we are passing through a worldwide COVID-19 pandemic, also more civil unrest in America, which fifty years from now will be long past. But preaching today, much of it online, will still have something to say to future generations. If this preaching is a genuine dialogue with truths expressed in Scripture, with valued traditions of the church, and with what is happening in our world, it will not be irrelevant to our grandchildren and great-grandchildren. We learn from history, and can learn from sermons preached at earlier times.

Scriptural quotations are largely from the New Revised Standard Version. Some are from the Revised Standard Version or the Anchor Bible, and a few are my own.

—Jack R. Lundbom

Introduction

James Muilenburg wrote in his little classic, *The Way of Israel*:

> The primary image to express conduct or behavior in the Old Testament is the "way" or "road" (*derek*). No other image was more rich and manifold, none more diverse in nuance and connotation . . . The way of a man was the course he followed through life, the direction of his going, and the manner of his walking. It was a good word because it was drawn from the vicissitudes of daily life, from a land of many roads and paths in which walking was the usual manner of going from one place to another. It was a good symbol because it involved beginning and end and the intention which prompted the journey. There were different ways a man might take, and his journey involved decision or choice of the right or the wrong road.[1]

"Walking in the way" has strong ethical implications in the Old Testament, especially in Deuteronomy, where the image applies broadly to the whole of life, whether of individuals or the Israelite nation. Walking in Yahweh's way translates into loving, serving, and fearing Yahweh, above all in keeping the commandments (Deut 5:33; 6:7; 8:6; 10:12; 11:19, 22; and so forth).

The Old Testament contains numerous teachings on the "two ways." In Deuteronomy Moses says at the close of a covenant renewal ceremony that people have two ways to walk: one leading to life, the other to death. The way to life is obeying the commandments; the way to death is disobeying them (Deut 30:15–20). The former brings blessing, the latter a curse. When Joshua renews the covenant at Shechem, the choice put before Israel is whether it will serve Yahweh or other gods (Joshua 24). Jeremiah later appropriates the Deuteronomic teaching in his two-way sermon of Jer

---

1. James Muilenburg, *The Way of Israel: Biblical Faith and Ethics* (New York: Harper & Row, 1961), 33.

Introduction

21:8–10, where the way to life is surrender to the Babylonians, and the way to death holding out in Jerusalem (cf. Jer 38:2, 17–18; 42:7–22).

In one Jeremiah oracle Yahweh has told people to stand where the roads intersect and seek out the ancient paths. Should they locate the good way, they will find rest. But they say, "We will not walk" (Jer 6:16). Because people gave no heed to this word, Yahweh will place before them stumbling blocks so they will fall (6:21). Other two-way teachings appear in wisdom literature (e.g., Ps 1; Prov 2).

Jesus teaches about two ways in his Sermon on the Mount, where the gate is narrow and the road hard that leads to life, and the gate wide and the road easy that leads to destruction (Matt 7:13–14). Two-way teachings have turned up at Qumran (4Q473),[2] appearing also in the pseudepigraphal literature (*Slav. En.* 30:15; *4 Ezra* 7:3–15; *T. Abr.* 11; *T. Ash.* 1:3–9) and in other Jewish and early Christian literature.[3]

If in the Old Testament life is described as walking down the good or right path, for Paul it is a race run in a stadium. To the Galatians he says, "You were running well; who hindered you from obeying the truth?" (Gal 5:7), and when nearing the end of his own life, Paul writes to Timothy: "I have fought the good fight, I have finished the race, I have kept the faith. From now on there is reserved for me the crown of righteousness" (2 Tim 4:7–8).

The greatest work of religious fiction in the English language is *Pilgrim's Progress*, an allegory on the Christian life by John Bunyan (b. 1628), written when the Puritan spirit was strong in England. Pilgrim sets out from the wilderness of this world for the World to Come; and on the journey meets Evangelist, Obstinate and Pliable; wallows in the Slough of Despond; meets Worldly Wiseman; is diverted to Legality's House; enters the Gate; and before the cross has the burden loosed from his back to go tumbling into the tomb; he sees it no more. At the end his rags are stripped from him and he is given new clothing. Sins are forgiven and peace is his.

John Wesley (b. 1703) talks about the narrow road to heaven being the way of lowliness, mourning, meekness, holy desire, love of God and one's

---

2. George J. Brooke et al., *Qumran Cave 4: XVII, Parabiblical Texts, Part 3*, Discoveries in the Judean Desert 22 (Oxford: Clarendon, 1996), 292–94.

3. Jack R. Lundbom, *Jesus' Sermon on the Mount: Mandating a Better Righteousness* (Minneapolis: Fortress, 2015), 257–59.

neighbor, doing good, and suffering evil for Christ's sake, the very things lifted up in Jesus' Sermon on the Mount.[4]

Swedish hymnody of the eighteenth and nineteenth centuries contains many hymns on life as a journey. "Chosen Seed and Zion's Children" (Lammets folk och Sions fränder), written by Anders Carl Rutström (b. 1721), has this for the first verse:

> Chosen seed and Zion's children
> Ransomed from eternal wrath
> Trav'ling to the heav'nly Canaan
> On a rough and thorny path
> Church of God in Christ elected
> You to God are reconciled
> But on earth you are a stranger
> Persecuted and reviled.[5]

Swedish Pietists also sang "As Pilgrims in This World" (Vi bo ej här), written by O. A. Ottander (1876), two verses of which are:

> As pilgrims in this world where life is fleeting
> We journey on to meet our dearest Friend
> Keep thou, O Lord, our hearts from false affections
> And lead us onward to the journey's end.
>
> Well may you ask if I can now be truly
> A child of God, the Lord's devoted bride
> But here you see in me my human frailties [Swedish: "now in my traveling clothes"]
> Some day you'll see my spirit glorified [Swedish: "in my beautiful bridal attire"].[6]

Judeo-Christian religion thus depicts life as walking down a path. Scripture fills out the image by telling us of a God hidden and revealed, and for Christians of Jesus lowly and exalted. For those making the Christian

---

4. John Wesley, *A Caution against False Prophets: A Sermon (Matt vii. 15–20)* (London: New Chapel and at Mr. Wesley's Preaching Houses in Town and Country, 1789), 4–5.

5. *The Covenant Hymnal: A Worshipbook* (Chicago: Covenant Publications, 1996), #421; translated by Claude W. Foss. Swedish original is found in *SionHarpan* (Chicago: Mission Friend's Publishing, 1890), #354.

6. *The Hymnal of the Evangelical Covenant Church of America* (Chicago: Covenant Press, 1950), #502; translated by Obed Johnson. Swedish original is found in *SionHarpan* (Chicago: Mission Friend's Publishing, 1890), #302.

Introduction

walk, it is necessary to understand it, discover how to be faithful in undertaking it, learn about stages in the walk, and finally, be instructed by wisdom themes, one of the most important being that foolishness is next to godlessness in preventing travelers from arriving at their destination.

Abbreviations

AB	The Anchor Bible
DDR	Deutsche Demokratische Republik
JB	The Jerusalem Bible
KJV	The King James Version
LXX	The Greek Septuagint
NRSV	The New Revised Standard Version
RSV	The Revised Standard Version

Walking with a Hidden and Revealed God

1

"I Will Be What I Will Be"[1]

Text: Exodus 3:11-14

But Moses said to God, "Who am I that I should go to Pharaoh, and bring the Israelites out of Egypt?" He said, "I will be with you; and this shall be the sign for you that it is I who sent you: when you have brought the people out of Egypt, you shall worship God on this mountain." But Moses said to God, "If I come to the Israelites and say to them, 'The God of your ancestors has sent me to you,' and they ask me, 'What is his name?' what shall I say to them? God said to Moses, "I will be what I will be."[2] He said further, "Thus you shall say to the Israelites, 'I WILL BE has sent me to you.'"

This passage in Exodus 3 is one you all know. It is that great text where God reveals himself to Moses in the burning bush, and then goes on to give him his name. Or does he? Scholars have labored over this text, some concluding that God does not give Moses his name; in fact, he avoids doing so. The key verse is v. 14, where God says to Moses, "I am who I am," or "I will be what I will be," and then follows with "Thus you shall say to the

---

1. Preached at the Beulah Covenant Church, Turlock, California, on February 26, 1978.

2. Hebrew אֶהְיֶה is translated in the verse as "I will be / I WILL BE" (RSV and NRSV footnote), not as "I am / I AM." The Septuagint has Ἐγώ εἰμι ὁ ὤν ("I am He Who Is" [JB] or "I am the Being One"). It takes the idiom as the divine name, which it is not. The KJV and more recent English Versions (RSV; NRSV) also take the idiom as the divine name, but the divine name is only the subsequent I WILL BE, which in v. 15 is changed to HE WILL BE (YHWH).

Israelites, 'I AM [or I WILL BE] has sent me to you.'" The next verse puts the Hebrew verb in the third person: YHWH, i.e., "HE IS" or "HE WILL BE," today vocalized as "Yahweh." Pious Jews later considered this name so sacred that they would not pronounce it; they therefore substituted "Lord." The tradition continues in virtually all modern Bible translations, from the King James Version on, where in place of the ineffable divine name the text reads, "The LORD" ("LORD" being in all capital letters). But the Jerusalem Bible, a very fine Roman Catholic Version, uses "Yahweh." At an earlier time, the divine name was vocalized "Jehovah," which we now know to be entirely wrong. Even Luther did not know this was a misreading of the Hebrew Bible.

I should mention that the reason for uncertainty about whether to translate "I am what I am" or "I will be what I will be" is that the Hebrew expression can be translated either present or future. Both would be right. The RSV and NRSV put the future in a footnote.

Today we know more about the idiom, which is common to Hebrew and Arabic. It occurs also in modern English. The idiom is given the Latin name *idem per idem*, which is a tautology used when one does not want to be more specific. Some other examples from the Old Testament:

> Jacob says to his sons when they tell him it is necessary to take Benjamin to Egypt: "If I am bereaved of my children, I am bereaved" (Gen 43:14);
>
> Moses tells the Israelites on the day before the sabbath: "Bake what you want to bake and boil what you want to boil" (Exod 16:23);
>
> David tells Ittai the Gittite, who wants to follow him into exile: "I will go where I will go" (2 Sam 15:20); and
>
> Esther, when she decides to approach the Persian king unannounced, says: "If I perish I perish" (Esth 4:16).

We use the idiom today:

> Boys will be boys
>
> Rules are rules
>
> The law is the law
>
> A rose is a rose is a rose (Gertrude Stein)

My father resorted to this idiom every now and then. He would say:

"I Will Be What I Will Be"

Do what you have to do

We're going where we're going

And that's that!

A popular song some years back made use of a Spanish proverb that was an *idem per idem*. A young girl asked her mother questions about the future, such as, "Will I be pretty?" and "Will I be rich?" to which the mother replied, "Que sera sera, whatever will be will be." And then there was Popeye, who at the end of his cartoons would say, "I yam what I yam and tha's all I yam, I'm Popeye the sailor man."

We have come also to realize that this idiom can have a definite function in discourse. It is a "conversation stopper," or if a debate is being carried on, it terminates the debate:

> When my father said, "We're going where we're going," he was terminating a debate on where we would go on our Sunday afternoon drive in the car;
>
> When he said, "And that's that," it terminated whatever debate we were having. I could say nothing more;
>
> If a student should happen to petition the dean at school about having a requirement waived, and the dean said, "But rules are rules," the student's plea was terminated;
>
> If a judge tells the defendant in court that "the law is the law," the case is closed;
>
> Even the mother in our song gently seeks to end the many questions her little girl is asking.

Another example of this idiom terminating debate occurs in the New Testament. Pilate has been arguing with the Jews about what to do with Jesus. After handing Jesus over to be crucified, he had an inscription written and put on the cross reading, "Jesus of Nazareth, the King of the Jews." But the chief priests objected: "Do not write 'The King of the Jews,' but, 'This man said, I am King of the Jews'" (John 19:22). Pilate then says, "What I have written I have written." He had enough; that was it. The debate was over.

Let us return to Exodus 3. There God is having a debate with Moses. He has decided to redeem his people from slavery and wants Moses to go to Pharaoh to see it carried out. Moses does not want to go. He says, "Who am I that I should go to Pharaoh, and bring the Israelites out of Egypt?" God responds, "I will be with you" (v. 12), which is his preeminent promise in the Bible. The Hebrew "I will be" is the same word that occurs in v. 14. Moses still is not persuaded. He says if he goes to the Israelites they will want to know God's name. Then God says, "I will be what I will be;" tell them "I WILL BE has sent me to you."

Now what is going on here? Quite simply this. God has said all he is going to say, and will only repeat himself. He has just told Moses, "I will be with you," so now he says "I will be what I will be," which terminates the debate. Moses says no more. In v. 12 everyone translates the verb a future; thus the verbs of the idiom in v. 14 must also be translated future, since v. 14 repeats v. 12.

We learn from this that while our God reveals himself at the same time he remains hidden. Tension between the two must be preserved lest the dynamic quality of biblical revelation be destroyed. Paul Ricoeur says:

> The idea of something secret is the limit-idea of revelation. The idea of revelation is a twofold idea. The God who reveals himself is a hidden God and hidden things belong to him . . . And in this regard nothing is as significant as the episode of the burning bush in Exodus 3. Tradition has quite rightly named this episode the revelation of the divine name. For this name is unnamable.[3]

Something similar happens in Exodus 33, where God and Moses are again in debate. This time, however, their positions are reversed: Moses is committed to the journey, but after the Golden Calf episode, God does not want to go along. Instead he offers to send his angel (32:34). But Moses will not hear of it; he says God himself must come. Finally God agrees, saying his presence (lit. his "face") will go. But Moses continues to press, asking to see God's glory, which refers to God's bright beneficent face. Once again he has asked too much. God answers:

> I will make all my goodness pass before you, and will proclaim before you my name, "The LORD;"[4] but I will be gracious to whom I will be gracious, and will show mercy on whom I will show mercy. Thus he said, "You cannot see my face, for no one shall see me and live" (Exod 33:19–20).[5]

---

3. Paul Ricoeur, "Toward a Hermeneutic of the Idea of Revelation," *HTR* 70 (1977), 17–18.

4. Hebrew has the unpronounceable YHWH (NRSV footnote).

5. Translation is my own.

"I Will Be What I Will Be"

God will let Moses see only his back as he passes by. A second time Moses has been silenced; this same idiom has terminated the debate.

We are faced, however, with a possible theological problem. For one on the receiving end of such an abrupt termination it is a less than satisfying experience. People resorting to this type of argument leave you feeling as if you have not really been answered. It seems high-handed, even irrational. On the human level, then, such an answer will be perceived as a non-answer. But can God argue in this manner?

Here, however, there is no problem, the reason being that God in both arguments is dispensing grace—in Exodus 3 he intends to deliver Israel out of a miserable slavery, and in Exodus 33 the discussion itself revolves around grace and mercy. God can be perfectly irrational—if we may use that term—in dispensing grace. He need not be, but often is. But when it comes to dispensing judgment, you will not hear the God of Israel say, "I will judge whomever I will judge." This is the way capricious gods of other religions act, explaining why people fear them so. In judgment our God always gives a reason.

We learn this in examining oracles of the prophets. When God indicts and judges people—also Israel and the nations—he has a reason for doing so. With Israel it is usually for breaking the covenant, which includes the Ten Commandments, or for violating laws of justice, ignoring commands to show benevolence to the needy, or for a host of other wrongdoings specified in the law. With other nations it is for unspeakable crimes against humanity (Amos 1:3–2:3), or because the nations are wicked, proud, and trusting in their own gods (Jer 25:31; 50:31–32, 38; 51:47, 52). However, when God gives Israel oracles of salvation, which abound in the latter chapters of Isaiah, see if you can find a reason. He acts to save because he acts to save. And who is going to complain if God wants to do good—for you, for a people, for the church, for the world?

An irrational God of grace is similarly portrayed in the New Testament. In the parable of the laborers in the vineyard (Matt 20:1–16), the giving of equal wages for unequal amounts of work seems eminently unfair, and the laborers who worked all day know it is unfair. But the landowner has great resources, and can be as generous as he wants. It is so with God. His resources are limitless and his grace boundless. He does not need a reason for being generous.

We can learn a lesson here from God. In indictments and judgments we need to be honest, rational, and fair. But when it comes to dispensing grace, or favor—which translates the same Hebrew word—we can be as generous as we want. We can give alms to the poor, food to the beggar, love to our enemies, and much, much more.

There is a second point I wish to lift up from our passage in Exodus 3, and with it I will close. The important verse is v. 12, where God tells Moses "I will be with you." This is God's preeminent promise, given on other occasions to Jacob (Gen 28:15), Joshua (Josh 1:5), Gideon (Judg 6:16), Jeremiah (Jer 1:8, 19; 15:20), and the Servant of Second Isaiah (Isa 41:10; 43:5). From Matthew in the New Testament we learn also that Jesus is called Emmanuel, "God with us" (Matt 1:23; 28:20).

AMEN

2

The Injustice in Divine Grace[1]

Text: Luke 15:29-30

But he answered his father, "Listen! For all these years I have been working like a slave for you, and I have never disobeyed your command; yet you have never given me even a young goat so that I might celebrate with my friends. But when this son of yours came back, who has devoured your property with prostitutes, you killed the fatted calf for him!"

Mbote!

Just six weeks ago we were celebrating the return of American hostages from Tehran. We watched on the television as they arrived in Algeria, then in Weisbaden, and finally in the United States. What followed was an outpouring of affection by an entire nation. It was good.

At about the same time I got a different slant on things as I sat in a medical office and heard a young woman pour out her heart. She watched the same television coverage, and had seen what the rest of us had seen, but instead of being joyous, she was bitter. Why did they get a parade, a host of yellow ribbons, and a visit to the White House? Prisoners who endured the jails of Viet Nam got none of this. And why did wives of the hostages get money to have their hair done in preparation for reunion with their husbands? Did the wives of those who fought in Iwo Jima get this? These hostages were complaining that the Iranians could only cook six American

---

1. Preached at the Communauté Evangélique de l'Ubangi-Mongala Church in Bokonjo, Zaire [Congo], on August 2, 1981. Translated by the Reverend Marvin Wickstrom into Lingala.

meals. What about prisoners for longer periods who received not even one American meal? This woman could not join in the celebration. It was all very unfair.

Some veterans of Viet Nam have also expressed bitterness this past week about what they have seen. "Look at the treatment they got compared to what we got," said one soldier from Oklahoma. Another from Michigan wrote this poem:

> O when will this country open its eyes
> And recognize the Viet Nam's veteran's cries
> No waving flags, no ticker tape parades
> You use your own people for your political charades

Here was more than personal hurt; there was the cynical suggestion that an entire nation was engaged in a big political game. These people were speaking about the injustice, the unfairness of it all. Were these hostages any better than others who suffered in war? And should a generation show unbridled affection one time when it failed to show it another time? They have a point.

The elder brother in Jesus' parable of the Prodigal Son also has a point. His father never gave him a kid so he could throw a feast and make merry with friends. So he is unable to join in the merriment for his younger brother. He can only focus on how deserving he has been. For a moment, at least, his life is stopped. He is expected to go in, but he adamantly refuses. The father pleads with him to join in the celebration. Did he finally go in? We don't know. The parable is said to be deliberately without an ending.

Among the many teachings in this parable is a very important one about grace—the father's grace, and God's grace. We see how unjust, how unfair, grace can be. The elder brother is no less sensitive to this than the woman I heard in the medical office or the vets unable to celebrate the return of the hostages.

Gifts of grace bestowed on us by others and by God are not dispensed equally. There are times when we, too, can say, "I never received that honor, that opportunity, or that special favor." There is the man unable to congratulate a colleague on a job promotion; he did not get the promotion he wanted; what is more, the last time he did get a promotion, no one shook his hand. There is the woman who will not go to a baby shower to see a friend's new baby. She wanted a baby, but could not have one; or perhaps she did have a baby, and no one gave her a shower. There is the person who will not support a scholarship appeal of his school. He did not get

The Injustice in Divine Grace

a scholarship when he went there; his family had to pay tuition, and he worked to pay his other expenses.

Underlying such attitudes are two beliefs: 1) that gifts must be given out equally; and 2) that one cannot give unless one has first received; if one did not get a party, why should he or she go to someone else's party? Both beliefs fail to understand what grace is all about—grace shown by other people, by a community, by a nation, by God.

Grace is a gift, and gifts are rarely given out equally. They do not have to be. Situations are different; generations are different; people are different. Modern psychologists, I believe, are partly responsible for telling us that a person is unable to give unless they have first received. A father unable to give love to his child is found not to have received love from his parent; a woman who could not love her father is now unable to love her husband. Doubtless there are cases such as these. But there are also "elder brothers." What I am saying is that these responses need not be. We can go to a party even if we have not had a party of our own.

Why? Because no one springs from a situation of such poverty that they have failed to experience grace. Usually we are talking about isolated events, which may be where the problem lies. I believe the elder brother when he says he has served his father loyally and done his bidding. Why not? Must we assume he has always exploded the way he is exploding now? Of course not. I also believe the father when he affirms the elder brother. It is obvious that the father has deep affection also for this son; over the years he has loved him and shown him favor.

It is simply that one event has brought into bold relief the injustice in grace. The son who was a scoundrel is given a party when he comes home; the faithful son never had one. Is there some injustice in it all? Yes. But Jesus tells the parable to show how grace breaks the bounds of human reason and strict justice when a father is overjoyed that a lost son has come home.

The parable is to teach us about God's dealings with us. We must know that divine grace can also be irrational and unjust just like human grace. It need not be, but it can be. God says to Moses, "I will be gracious to whom I will be gracious, and I will show mercy on whom I will show mercy" (Exod 33:19).

Other parables of Jesus convey the same truth. There is the parable of the talents, where one fellow gets five talents, another three, and another one (Matt 25:14–30). Why the inequity? Another parable likely to rankle those who think everything must be given out equally is the parable of the

Laborers in the Vineyard, where those hired at the eleventh hour get the same money as those working the whole day (Matt 20:1–16). Once again, our God is a gracious God and can give more if he so chooses. And sometimes he does choose to give more. In this latter parable there is also no injustice in that the laborers working all day were given exactly what was promised.

We must come to terms with a God who dispenses grace with liberality. He does not want us crying like spoiled children because we did not get this or did not get that, or did not get what someone else received. Also, we must rid ourselves of the notion that we cannot give unless we have first received. The truth is we have all been showered throughout life with divine grace, and from that reservoir we can give to others whatever the situation may be. Life itself is a divine gift; and the individual blessings we have received are numberless. At the root of our problem is selfishness, pride, and ingratitude. AMEN

3

"No Other Name"[1]

Transfiguration

Text: Acts 4:12

There is salvation in no one else, for there is no other name under heaven given among mortals by which we must be saved.

Years ago in our North Park Hi-League we would go around the room during one of our meetings and each person would be asked to give his or her favorite Bible verse. When it came to my turn I would almost always recite the verse I have chosen as my text for this morning, which is Transfiguration Sunday. We could recite Bible verses from memory in those days, and it would be from the only English Bible we knew: the King James Version.

I have chosen this text today because it says very concisely what the Christian Church has long said about Jesus, namely, that his name is the only name whereby people may be saved, but also because it provides an excellent summation of the event Luke reports in his Gospel about the Transfiguration (Luke 9:28–36). It is one of the best early commentaries on that event. The incomparable name of Jesus is the only name whereby we may be saved.

---

1. Preached at the North Park Covenant Church, Chicago, on February 9, 1986.

For many today it would be enough to say that Jesus has a name. Maybe they would even know that Jesus translates the Hebrew Joshua, a name we also remember. Having a name can signify preeminence, which only a select few attain. There are famous names in all fields—politics, sports, the arts, the media, in the world, and so forth.

The Chicago Bears again have a name—although one might dispute as to whether it is an altogether good one. I remember when the Bears were the biggest winners in football, and I heard stories as a boy of how they used to be even greater. I heard about Bronko Nagurski, who had a name bigger than life. I was so excited to see to see him, now an old man, flip the coin a year ago at the Super Bowl. I saw his short legs, and know how be became such a great runner. He was a hard man to tackle.

In our own Covenant Church are people with a name: David Nyvall, Nils Lund, J. A. Hultman, Peter Matson, Warner Sallman, Karl Olsson, and others. Some were members of this church. Names are a mark of preeminence.

In the Bible we find it no less true that certain names stand out. There were the Patriarchs, Abraham, Isaac, and Jacob; there was Moses; Kings Saul, David, and Solomon; there was Job and Daniel, both known now from ancient Ugaritic texts to have been men of renown. There were the prophets, Samuel, Elijah, Elisha, Amos, Hosea, Micah, Isaiah, Jeremiah, Ezekiel, and others, who despite shameful treatment in their own time achieved greatness in later tradition.

Moses and Elijah were two of the greatest individuals in the Old Testament. Deuteronomy portrays Moses as prophet par excellence—greater even than Elijah, who performed mighty works, and greater than prophets of the eighth century, who had attained preeminence among the people (Deut 34:10–12). But Elijah assumes great importance in later Jewish tradition. He ascended into heaven (2 Kgs 2:9–12), and will return, according to the prophet Malachi, to usher in the coming day of the Lord (Mal 4:5–6). In Jewish tradition Elijah is also the one who will come to decide difficult matters no one else can decide. At the conclusion of every Passover Seder Meal, a child is sent to open the door in a symbolic anticipation of Elijah's return.

Now as the ministry of Jesus is coming to a grand climax and Jesus is on his way to Jerusalem, the Gospel writers weave a series of events into their narratives to indicate how people were coming to ask who this Jesus was. It should impress us that a right question was being asked. Good questions are always better than mindless answers. Quite often when we read the Gospels, especially Mark, we come away thinking that the disciples didn't understand anything. It's not just Peter; all of them are pretty dense. Luke is more positive about Jesus' gradual self-disclosure.

Luke tells us at the beginning of chapter 9 that people were asking who Jesus was, and there was a diversity of opinion. Some said John the Baptist had been raised from the dead; others said he was Elijah who had returned; some mentioned names of other prophets. Even wily Herod Antipas entered the discussion. He was perplexed, which is one of the best things to say about this inept ruler. Having beheaded John the Baptist he could only say, "Who is this about whom I hear such things?"

A few verses later (9:18–20) Jesus puts the question to his disciples: "Who do the crowds say that I am?" Note it is the *who* question, not a question about divinity, humanity, or a *what* question about substance. Dietrich Bonhoeffer pointed out to us that the question of Jesus is a *who* question. The disciples repeat names currently being tossed about. But Peter confesses Jesus to be the Christ, that is, the Messiah. Following this is the Transfiguration account. In this grand vision given the disciples of Jesus—a vision that is really a "prefiguration" of the Jesus to be exalted after he has suffered and died—Moses and Elijah appear. They too appear in glory; their clothes and presence had a brilliance like the brilliance Jesus possessed. It appears as if a new star has been born, a new member elected to the heavenly hall of fame. We are quick to fault Peter for proposing that all three be given "dwellings," which must have been an oblique way of wanting Moses, Elijah, and Jesus all to be given prominence.

Luke tells us that Peter did not know what he was saying. Probably he didn't. But Peter may have been seeking to bring the others to a new level of understanding by acknowledging that Jesus deserved to be ranked with two of the greatest individuals in Jewish tradition. Then we come to the climax of the event. A cloud covers them and the voice of God is heard. The "who" question is answered. God says, "This is my Son, my Chosen; listen to him" (9:35).

These words are enough for us to know that Jesus is not simply someone with a name; he is not one who is preeminent along with other preeminent individuals; he is someone set apart, unlike all others. His name is like no other name. The fading of Moses and Elijah confirm this. When Luke concludes, "Jesus was found alone," this says it all. Jesus is the only Son of the one God, as John puts it in his Gospel. He is the name—the only name—by which men and women can be saved. We are expected to be as single-minded about this Jesus as the Jews were about Yahweh when they recited words of the Shema in Deut 6:4.

This is the first point I want to make this morning. We are living in a day when a host of religious traditions are flourishing, and the emphasis is on pluralism. I have always believed that we should be respectful of other religious traditions, to learn as much as we can about them, and be charitable towards people of other traditions, but for the Christian Jesus alone is at the center of our faith. He is at the center in Paul's preaching and at the center of every other NT writing. We need then to balance off our single devotion to Christ with an open mind to other traditions, traditions infinitely more complex and about which opinions widely differ.

Simplistic extensions and substitutes of this great confession can cause problems. I refer to the tendency to be single-minded about a host of other things—some being of lesser importance, some digressing markedly from the view that Jesus is the only name to be worshiped, some that are a part of our cultural and intellectual heritage, and some that are outright perversions. We must always be careful of single-mindedness about a certain doctrine, a certain view of biblical inspiration, and single-mindedness about other subjects, e.g., views of human development, philosophic views, psychological views on how to raise a family, how to treat one's husband or wife, adopting a certain lifestyle, et cetera.

It is no accident that we are repulsed by single-mindedness of some people, maybe even family members or close friends. We call it narrow-mindedness" or close-mindedness, which takes a variety of shapes and forms. Mothers think that because their child acts a certain way, all children act that way—although this can change when a second child comes along. Even so, the broadness and complexity of human behavior is often not fully understood. We had people in this church years ago who were single-minded about Buick automobiles, as if there were no other car to drive. As a boy, I took notice when our recently arrived pastor came driving down Berwyn Avenue in a new Buick.

Some of the most ridiculous reductions are made today by Christian people, e.g., that being Christian means eating a certain health food or using a certain cosmetic. I have met some who argue that because the Holy Spirit inspires Scripture there can be no imperfections in the biblical text. Such people know nothing about ancient texts and their history of transmission. They know nothing about manuscripts found at Qumran. Many have never heard of the Greek Old Testament, the Septuagint, which every

"No Other Name"

modern Bible—including the King James Version—follows at some point. It has many different readings than the Hebrew text. What I am saying is that singlemindedness about Jesus should not make us single-minded about too many other things, although a single view on some things is right and good.

In the New Testament no one is more single-minded about Jesus Christ than the Apostle Paul, and yet on many other things he is as pluralistic as can be. Paul had to be open-minded if he was to be a missionary to the Gentiles, which he was with great success. Paul helped negotiate key issues with James and the apostles at the Jerusalem Conference reported in Acts 15, where he agreed not to require circumcision for Gentiles. Yet he did circumcise Timothy (Acts 16:3). But he accepted at this conference that Gentiles be required to follow two points of the Jewish law: not to eat what was strangled, and not to eat the blood. And we know, do we not, how Paul was "flip-flop" about the law. He claimed to uphold it, but did not uphold all the 613 laws taught by the Pharisees.

There is a second point I want to make about the preeminence of Jesus, one that is brought into bold relief in the verses following our text. The exalted Christ reduces the profile of all who are Christ's disciples. It is not only other preeminent individuals who fade away in the cloud; the disciples too must fade away. Luke says the very next day an argument broke out among the disciples as to who was the greatest (9:46–48). If Jesus was to have a preeminent place in the kingdom of God, might not they also have positions of preeminence? They were Jesus' closest disciples. People reason the same way today. If you are a close supporter of an emerging leader, might you not jockey for position if that person succeeds in becoming the leader? But Jesus has another lesson to teach the disciples. No one among his disciples must be bigger than life. Greatness comes in being humble, becoming like a little child, being least in order that one day you may be great. This is something different from putting yourself forward as a somebody!

Let me close with a personal experience. I left North Park almost twenty years ago to study Old Testament with Dr. James Muilenburg, one of America's preeminent biblical scholars. Fred Holmgren of this congregation had studied with him, and because of my regard for this teacher in our seminary, I decided I too wanted to be a student of Dr. Muilenburg.

When I arrived in San Anselmo, California, to do my doctoral work, I soon discovered that Dr. Muilenburg had a wonderful way of making you feel that you were special. When you were talking to him it was as if you were the only person that mattered. So as time went on, I began to feel that I had become a special student of his. Well, in talking to fellow students I discovered that they too felt as if they were special students of Dr. Muilenburg. Maybe he had more than one special student. After graduating and beginning to teach, and moving about more broadly, I met up with other former students of Dr. Muilenburg, and it was incredible: just about everyone thought of himself or herself as Dr. Muilenburg's special student. They had the same feeling I had! I am happy to tell you that no dispute has broken out as to who was the greatest. We were all great, and that was enough from a teacher who was himself great. AMEN

4

O Jerusalem, Jerusalem:
You Spared Jeremiah—But Thanks Be to God![1]

Text: Jeremiah 40:1–6

The word that came to Jeremiah from the Lord *after Nebuzaradan the captain of the guard had let him go from Ramah, when he took him bound in fetters along with all the captives of Jerusalem and Judah who were being exiled to Babylon. The captain of the guard took Jeremiah and said to him, "The* Lord *your God threatened this place with this disaster, and now the* Lord *has brought it about, and has done as he said, because all of you sinned against the* Lord *and did not obey his voice. Therefore this thing has come upon you. Now look, I have just released you today from the fetters on your hands. If you wish to come with me to Babylon, come, and I will take good care of you; but if you do not wish to come with me to Babylon, you need not come. See, the whole land is before you; go wherever you think it good and right to go. If you remain, then return to Gedaliah son of Ahikam son of Shaphan, whom the king of Babylon appointed governor of the towns of Judah, and stay with him among the people; or go wherever you think it right to go. So the captain of the guard gave him an allowance of food and a present, and let him go. Then Jeremiah went to Gedaliah son of Ahikam at Mizpah, and stayed with him among the people who were left in the land.*

---

1. Preached at the Lutheran Church of the Redeemer, Jerusalem, on November 16, 1997; also at St. Mark's Church, Cambridge, England, on March 8, 1998.

Oil Enough to Make the Journey

O Jerusalem, Jerusalem

An old city you are
Perched atop a Judean mountain
Known to the traders of Ebla
As Urusalima
Thirteen centuries before David
When Egypt was building pyramids

Melchizedek was your priest
In the time of Abraham
And through him an alliance was made
Between you and God Most High
Between your people and his people
They knew of you in Egypt
Long before Moses
When you bowed to the pharaohs
And to city-kings up north

Then David came
And like a bride
You became his very own
The Lord too made you his city
And came to rest in you
After a long and arduous journey
But it was left to Solomon
To dress you like the queen you were
Making you beautiful in cedar and stone
So nations would come to visit you
And they did—yes, they did

But your beauty you took too seriously
You forgot not only David
But also the Lord your God
And so your high stone walls
And your tunnels bringing water from Siloam
Were protection only for a time
Micah said they would plow you as a field
But the people listened rather to Isaiah
Who said the Assyrians could not take you
And they didn't
But they cooped up the good Hezekiah
Like a bird in a cage

O JERUSALEM, JERUSALEM:

You were inviolable
So you thought
Until the time of Jeremiah
When you heard the word of the Lord
In such clarity and power
You could not stand it
And you became hostile and ugly
When he said you would fall
But you fell
And the great Babylonian king
Burned your forests of cedar
And tore down your stone mountains
And the people who were your flesh and blood
He left for dead or took away

O Jerusalem, Jerusalem
City of glory
City of shame
The whole world has seen both
And cannot forget you.[2]

Perhaps it was due to strong religious beliefs in the south, fed by traditions about Abraham and David, preserved first at Hebron and later in Jerusalem, that Jerusalem came to think of itself as being special. Covenants made with Abraham and David carried with them no conditions; they were irrevocable and for all time. Jerusalem had the idea that God had also chosen her for all time. This belief is expressed in a psalm:

> For the LORD has chosen Zion
>   he has desired it for his habitation
> "This is my resting place forever
>   here I will reside, for I have desired it
> I will abundantly bless its provisions
>   I will satisfy its poor with bread
> Its priests I will clothe with salvation
>   and its faithful will shout for joy
> There I will cause a horn to sprout up for David
>   I have prepared a lamp for my anointed one
> His enemies I will clothe with disgrace
>   but on him, his crown will gleam.
> (Ps 132:13–18)

2. Published subsequently in my *Jeremiah 37–52* (AB 21C; New York: Doubleday, 2004), 94–95.

But like all other cities Jerusalem became a dwelling for evil. And so the Lord raised up prophets who had the unhappy task of calling this evil to the city's attention and clarify its muddled relationship with the Lord.

Schooled as they were in traditions about Moses, traditions preserved in the north but brought south after the Northern Kingdom fell in 722 BC, the prophets knew that the Lord's covenant with the land—including Jerusalem—was not as secure as his covenant with Israel. Deuteronomy taught that the covenant with the land was conditional: If Israel kept the commandments, she could stay in the land; if she did not, the Lord would drive her out.

It therefore fell to Jeremiah to tell the people that there was no more *if* about it. The covenant had been broken, and the land, city, temple, and nationhood would be destroyed. Survivors would be carried off into exile. Jeremiah was not a native of Jerusalem, but he lived his entire life in the shadow of and within this great city. He was born in the village of Anathoth, three miles to the north. Though close to the southern capital, Anathoth lay in Benjamin, which belonged to tribes of the north. Jeremiah was thus raised on northern traditions, influenced by Moses, Samuel, and the prophet Hosea.

One day, however, Jeremiah made his way to Jerusalem. We do not know when it was—perhaps he went to school there, studying with Shaphan at Jerusalem's school for priests and scribes. In any case, we find him preaching to people of the city when Josiah was king, in the courtyard of the temple, at one of the city gates, and anywhere people would stop to listen.

This became a "cross" for Jeremiah, for as time went on, he encountered the city's deep hostility. The Lord told him beforehand this would happen. The Lord was about to bring evil upon Jerusalem and all Judah, and Jeremiah must announce it (Jer 1:14–19). People, of course, would not want to hear it—preferring, as they always do, good news to bad—and they would vent their wrath on the one who spoke such things. In fact, people high and low would fight him, but the Lord said not to be afraid. He would make Jeremiah into a fortified city, an iron pillar, and bronze walls against all opposition. Despite their attacks, the Lord would be with him to deliver him.

This is the gospel of the Old Testament: the preservation of one of God's servants against all odds. Later God would bring life through death and after death, but for now it would be enough to preserve a chosen servant from death. That is the promise in the first chapter of the book of Jeremiah.

The book goes on to tell us just how this promise was kept. We have more biographical information about Jeremiah than about any other prophet. One reason, no doubt, is that Jeremiah's legacy was preserved by a professional Jerusalem scribe, Baruch son of Neriah. Another may be that Baruch wanted to relate the drama of how the Lord's promise to Jeremiah was fulfilled. It was not enough to listen to Jeremiah's oracles at the temple or in the streets, important as these were. We must also observe the man himself, living out a life of obedience to the Lord, suffering, and suffering some more, but in the end seeing the Lord's promise fulfilled.

Hostility began early, and it was close to home. Members of the prophet's family made a plot on his life, but it failed (Jer 11:18-23). From then on it was conflict with kings, priests, prophets, and leading citizens of Jerusalem. Pashhur the priest was the first to beat him and put him in stocks for the night. He had spoken out against Jerusalem in the Valley of Ben Hinnom and later in the courtyard of the temple (19:1—20:6).

When Jehoiakim became king, Jeremiah delivered his famous "temple oracles," warning of the temple's destruction (7:1-15; 26). When finished, Jeremiah was brought into a hastily convened court to hear fellow priests and prophets call for his death. Jeremiah defended himself by saying that the Lord had called him to prophesy, and in the end the princes and others on the jury accepted his testimony. Elders present at the trial also recalled Micah saying earlier that Jerusalem would be "plowed as a field" (Jer 26:18), and King Hezekiah did not put him to death. Jeremiah was then spared, although he needed subsequent the protection of his friend Ahikam (26:24).

In the fifth year of Jehoiakim, Baruch read a scroll of Jeremiah's oracles in the temple; Jeremiah himself could not read it for was debarred from entering the temple precinct. So he sent Baruch (36:4-8). The prophet's preaching caused such a stir that both Jeremiah and Baruch had to go into hiding, where they remained seven long years. The biblical writer says, "the Lord hid them" (36:26).

Zedekiah was then put on the throne by Nebuchadnezzar, who brought the city to its knees ten years before its final collapse. He took all the important people of the city into exile. For a brief time Jeremiah was now able to come out into the open. But not long after, he was arrested again and put into a dungeon. It seems he was leaving the city to go to

Anathoth to attend to family business, but the guard thought he was deserting to the Babylonians (37:11–16). King Zedekiah finally let him out of the pit when he was near death, placing him under house arrest (37:17–21). There he received a loaf of bread daily from Baker's Street until there was no more bread in the city.

Others in Jerusalem were hostile towards him, throwing him again into an empty cistern, where he sank in the mud (38:6). He would have died there, had it not been for Ebed-melech, a black man from Ethiopia in the employ of the king, who came to his aid. Together with others they pulled Jeremiah out of the pit by ropes.

Many times Jeremiah was close to death. But when the city was taken, and countless others were shown no mercy, Jeremiah received mercy— from the Babylonians, and from the Lord. Nebuchadnezzar personally gave orders to Nebuzaradan for his safety and welfare. "See, the whole land is before you," Nebuzaradan told him (Jer 40:4). The psalmist had said, "The meek shall inherit the land" (Ps 37:11), later repeated by Jesus in the Sermon on the Mount (Matt 5:5). O Jerusalem, Jerusalem, You spared Jeremiah, but thanks be to God! It was only by God's grace that you did not kill him as you did to so many other prophets (Matt 23:37).

On this first Sunday in Lent may we remember Jeremiah and the cross he bore, also what would have made that cross unnecessary: It would have been unnecessary if evil had not flourished and spiraled out of control; it would have been unnecessary had not beautiful people become ugly people overcome by evil.

Sin made the cross necessary, and we can see how sin makes people so vicious. In blindness they project their own evil on others better than themselves. But we learn from Jeremiah that the word of the Lord endures. It is a sure word when times are bad and seemingly hopeless. Evil has a life, but it is a short life. In the end it is defeated. Only the word of the Lord endures forever. AMEN

5

Scriptures and Bread Broken Open[1]

Easter

Text: Luke 24:28–35

As they came near the village to which they were going, he walked ahead as if he were going on. But they urged him strongly, saying, "Stay with us, because it is almost evening and the day is now nearly over." So he went in to stay with them. When he was at table with them, he took bread, blessed and broke it, and gave it to them. Then their eyes were opened, and they recognized him; and he vanished from their sight. They said to each other, "Were not our hearts burning within us while he was talking to us on the road, while he was opening the scriptures to us?" That same hour they got up and returned to Jerusalem; and they found the eleven and their companions gathered together. They were saying, "The Lord has risen indeed, and he has appeared to Simon!" Then they told what had happened on the road, and how he had been made known to them in the breaking of the bread.

If you were to visit Soviet Russia today, you might be able to see the body of Nikolai Lenin preserved in a mausoleum in Moscow. At certain times of the year people wait in long lines just to view it. It is true also in China, where

---

1. Preached at the Covenant Church in Thomaston, Connecticut, on April 3, 1983.

the body of Mao Zedong lies well-preserved. In antiquity the Egyptians were the experts in preserving bodies of the dead. We can see their mummies even today. And the great pyramids give visible testimony to worship of the dead in ancient Egypt.

There would be no such worship among the Israelites, who left Egypt for the land promised to Abraham, Isaac, and Jacob. When their leader Moses died, his burial place was kept secret. We read in the closing words of Deuteronomy: "And he buried him in the valley in the land of Moab opposite Beth-peor; but no man knows the place of his burial to this day" (Deut 34:6). The "he" has no antecedent, so the rabbis reverently explained that the Lord God buried him. Perhaps the Lord was also the one who made sure that no trace was left of his grave. Israelites would not worship a dead hero; they would worship a living God.

The burial place of Jesus was not kept secret, but we see the beginnings of a cult of the dead when women went to the tomb Easter morning. The spices and ointments had the smell of Egypt. Words of the angels were the words of God: "Why do you look for the living among the dead?" Did the women not know Jesus said that on the third day he would rise again? It was the third day. Nevertheless, when they heard this, they did remember Jesus' words and ran to tell the apostles, but they and those with them did not believe it. Luke goes on to report that remarkable incident where Jesus meets travelers on the Emmaus road. There would be no worship of the dead. No sooner had it begun it was ended. And early Christians became no more concerned about marking the tomb of Jesus than the Israelites were to mark Moses's burial place.

It was only in the fourth century AD, after Constantine made Christianity the religion of the Roman Empire, that people became interested in locating holy places. In 335 the Basilica of Constantine was built over the place thought to be Calvary and the tomb of Jesus. Today it is the Church of the Holy Sepulchre. Many of today's pilgrims to the Holy Land visit another site discovered by the British General Gordon in the last century (1867). It is the so-called Garden Tomb, where centuries ago an ancient church stood adjacent to it. It gives a good look of what Jesus' tomb must have looked like, but archaeologists have shown that this is probably not the site.

In any case, what the earliest Christians avoided has nevertheless come to be. At both sites, lines of people—many in tour groups—wait to see the presumed place where Jesus was buried. But here is the good news. They see no body. At the Church of the Holy Sepulchre they can do no more than

Scriptures and Bread Broken Open

bend down to kiss the marble. There and around the world Christians are celebrating that the tomb was empty and remained empty. Christ is risen!

When we read Luke's account more closely, we see that the empty tomb actually had little impact on those who first saw it. We mentioned how the women responded. They went to tell the apostles about Jesus' resurrection only after they remembered his words about rising on the third day. And when they did tell the apostles, the words seemed to them an "idle tale." Peter, after running to the tomb and finding it empty, went home amazed. The empty tomb was not decisive.

When the men on the Emmaus road recounted the day's happenings to their fellow traveler, they seemed unimpressed by the women's report of an empty tomb. Some of their number had gone to the tomb and found it just as the women had said, but they did not see Jesus. They were still looking sad. Actually, Luke is rather kind to the women. He credits them for remembering Jesus' words about rising on the third day, and says they did go and tell the apostles about what had happened. But they said only that they had seen angels who said Jesus was alive, and they had remembered Jesus' words, but Jesus they did not see.

In Mark's account, which we believe to be the earliest, the women do not come off nearly as good. Mark closes his Gospel saying, "So they went out and fled from the tomb, for terror and amazement had seized them; and they said nothing to anyone, for they were afraid" (Mark 16:8). No, a tomb broken open was not what brought Jesus' followers to faith. Not even the testimony of angels, which we learn from v. 23 came in a vision. It was a personal encounter with the risen Lord. Luke relates how travelers met him on the Emmaus road; John reports Jesus' appearance to Mary Magdalene in the garden, and Thomas believing only when Jesus met him behind closed doors and showed him his hands and side (John 20). Later, Paul will also meet the risen Christ on a road, this one going to Damascus.

It was no different for Martin Luther; or for Grandma and Grandpa, who encountered Jesus in a revival meeting a century ago. It takes a personal encounter with the risen Lord to bring one to faith. That must happen to each one of us. How does it happen? Well, in a number of ways. On the Emmaus road it happened in two important ways: Jesus was revealed to Cleopas and his friends in the breaking open of the Scriptures and in the breaking of the bread.

What a natural way for Jesus to reveal himself. All during his ministry he had been opening the Scriptures. He preached and taught regularly in the synagogue, and opened up the Scriptures on the hills of Galilee. Our Lord knew the Scriptures and taught the Scriptures. During these same years Jesus took time to eat with people. Sometimes it was in their homes; other times it was on the hillside. To feed people's minds is a high calling, but Jesus did not consider it beneath him to see that hungry mouths were filled with food. Who can forget the feeding of the five thousand? In his last hours with the disciples Jesus ate and drank at a Passover meal. Small wonder now that the travelers' hearts burned as he opened the Scriptures on the road, and then opened their eyes by breaking bread at the table in Emmaus.

So basic were these two manifestations of the risen Lord to early Christians that they became the main parts of worship: reading and interpreting the Scriptures, and celebrating Holy Communion (the Eucharist). Throughout the ages Christian worship has consisted of these two rites. In the Eastern Orthodox Church the high points are the Little Entrance and the Great Entrance. The Little Entrance is the bringing in of the Gospel; the Great Entrance bringing in the bread and wine.

The Roman Catholic Church has a Liturgy of the Word, which is the reading of Scripture and a homily (a sermon), and a Liturgy of the Eucharist. But over time the focus came largely to be on the Eucharist. The Protestant Reformation sought to redress this imbalance, reemphasizing the reading of Scripture and exposition of it in a sermon. Luther aided a focus on the Word by translating the Bible into German and teaching children a catechism. Now, after Vatican II, the Roman Catholic Church has more Scripture reading and homilies. In our own church we try to balance reading from the Bible, preaching, and Bible study, with Holy Communion and fellowship generally, which would include coffee, potlucks, and other social times around the table.

The goal of worship is to bring us into the presence of our risen Lord. We read the Bible not because it is an interesting and fascinating book, nor just to learn about Jewish and Christian religion. We do both, but we read it because it is God's Word; in it we come to know Jesus and find new life in him. We join in table fellowship to have a mysterious union with the risen Lord.

If you have not had a personal encounter with Jesus on some Emmaus road, I suggest you break open the Scriptures and let Jesus to speak to you. If more people today would do this, and do it with enthusiasm, we would have a revival on our hands. Secondly, we must discover, if we have not already done so, new ways of experiencing table fellowship—Christians

Scriptures and Bread Broken Open

with other Christians, and Christians with non-Christians. We had table fellowship last Thursday evening at church, and a rich experience it was. It would have been richer with double the number! Breaking bread, however, does not take place only in church. It occurs in our homes, in restaurants, or in open spaces when the weather turns warm. Jesus is risen! Where will you find him today? AMEN

6

"A God Far Off"[1]

Text: Jeremiah 23:23–24

*Am I a God near by, says the L*ORD*, and not a God far off? Who can hide in secret places so that I cannot see them? says the L*ORD*. Do I not fill heaven and earth? says the L*ORD*.*

The prophet Jeremiah, after censuring prophets who were running without being sent, poses a rhetorical question from God: "Am I a God near by and not a God far off?" Then follows a couple other rhetorical questions: "Who can hide in secret places so that I cannot see them? Do I not fill heaven and earth?" False prophets go hide when the enemy comes, and their words turn up empty. Many will not know where they are, but God knows; he sees in all the secret places.

Jeremiah had a similar word for priests and other worshipers in the temple. In the second of his celebrated temple oracles of 609 BC, he speaks to people who think they can steal, murder, commit adultery, swear, and burn incense to Baal, and then come into the Lord's house and say, "We are safe!" only to keep on doing these abominations. Has God's house has become a robber's den? If so, God says, "Look I have seen" (Jer 7:8–11 AB). God sees in the darkness.

When it comes to fleeing the all-seeing God of Israel, the psalmist says:
> Where can I go from your spirit?
>   or where can I flee from your presence?

1. Preached at the Covenant Church in Berkeley, California, on August 8, 1976.

"A God Far Off"

> If I ascend to heaven, you are there
> > if I make my bed in Sheol, you are there
>
> If I take the wings of the morning
> > and settle at the farthest limits of the sea
>
> Even there your hand shall lead me
> > and your right hand shall hold me fast
>
> If I say, "Surely the darkness shall cover me
> > and the light around me become night"
>
> Even the darkness is not dark to you
> > the night is as bright as the day
> > for darkness is as light to you.
>
> (Ps 139:7–12)

Amos knows this, warning about an ever-present God who will come in judgment (Amos 9:1–4). His prophecy is followed by a doxology extolling a God "who builds his upper chambers in the heavens, and founds his vault upon the earth" (vv. 5–6).

The Old Testament uses near and far imagery, immanence and transcendence, which are boundary terms, to describe God's location in relation to people, imagery not necessarily tied to judgment but used to teach a variety of things. The book of Deuteronomy, for the most part, situates God in heaven. After the worshiper has offered his charity tithe at the Feast of Booths, he concludes with a prayer to God: "Look down from your holy habitation, from heaven, and bless your people Israel and the ground that you have given us, as you swore to our ancestors—a land flowing with milk and honey" (Deut 26:15; cf. 4:36). However, when Israel is engaged in holy war, the camp must be ritually clean. Why? Because Yahweh God resides also on earth; he walks in the midst the camp, and if he sees anything indecent he will turn away (Deut 23:9–14; cf. 4:39).

Both near and far images of where God resides occur in Genesis. Jacob in his dream at Bethel sees a ladder from earth to heaven with angels ascending and descending. When he awakes he feels as if he had been at the gate of heaven (Gen 28:10–17). But in the story of Adam and Eve, after both had eaten the forbidden fruit they heard the sound of the Lord God walking in the garden in the cool of the day (Gen 3:8). No God in a distant heaven here!

The idea emerged after David conquered Jerusalem and Solomon built his temple that Zion had become the Lord's permanent dwelling place (Ps 132:13–14). The Lord would now be permanently "at hand." This idea lasted for years, but changed with the arrival of Nebuchadnezzar and the fall of Jerusalem. Ezekiel in a vision saw the glory of the Lord leaving Jerusalem in a chariot bound for Babylon (Ezek 11:22–23).

In the Old Testament generally, people are earthbound: they are born on earth, they live their lives on earth, and they die on earth, descending at death into a deep pit called Sheol. Elijah is the only person at the end to ride a chariot into heaven (2 Kings 2:11). The prophet Malachi says he will return to usher in the coming day of the Lord (Mal 4:5–6). But in later Judaism Moses is also thought to have ascended to heaven. This is recorded in a Jewish writing entitled *The Assumption of Moses*,[2] dating from about the first century AD. Enoch, too, who "walked with God and was no more because God took him" (Gen 5:24), became a traveler in the heavenly regions in a pseudepigraphal work dated ca. 250–150 BC (1 Enoch). From the New Testament we learn that Abraham, Isaac, Jacob, and all the prophets are in heaven (Matt 8:11; Luke 13:28; 16:19–31). In 1950 Pope Pius XII and the Roman Catholic Church issued a doctrine saying that Mary had been bodily assumed into heaven. I remember wondering at the time about this, but I shouldn't have. In 1957 my grandma died, and on that very day everyone in our family believed she went to heaven.

We learn from the New Testament that Jesus came from heaven to live among us. At his death he descended into the Dead, then rose again, after which he ascended into heaven (Luke 24:50–51; Mark 16:19; John 3:13; 20:17; Acts 1:9–11). Luke in Acts adds that he will come again. We affirm all this in the Apostles and Nicene Creeds. Matthew, however, has no ascension of Jesus into heaven. The reason may be that for this Gospel writer Jesus is Emmanuel, "God *with us*" (Matt 1:23), and Jesus' last words to the disciples is the Great Commission concluding: "Remember, *I am with you* always, to the end of the age" (Matt 28:20).

I think it fair to say that the most treasured testimony of the church is that our God comes near. We affirm this regarding God's sending of Jesus. And it happens often when people pray, when the church experiences a revival, or when other spiritual happenings take place. I have heard China missionaries exclaim after a revival broke out in one of their churches, "How wonderful it was! You could just sense God's presence / the Holy Spirit among us." Probably the reason we celebrate the nearness of God is that we know he is not always near. Sometimes he seems very far away. When tragedies occur, someone can be heard crying, "Where is God?" This happened during the Holocaust, and it has happened many other times.

---

2. Also called *The Testament of Moses*.

"A God Far Off"

I must confess, however, that for me it is a comfort when a dear one dies that I can put my trust in a God far off. I remember feeling this way when our little girl not yet two years old died suddenly of a virus. We said our last goodbyes in this church. I felt then as if God was far off, because our little girl was far off. I had known times when God felt near, but not now. When we returned home, and it came time for her three-year-old brother to say bedtime prayers, we had to make a change. It was now "bless baby Joan who is in heaven with Jesus."

Knowing a God far off might be a good corrective, and if not a corrective certainly a balancing affirmation, to a theology of immanence about which we hear so much today. Paul Tillich wants to make God "the Ground of all Being," which no Israelite would have understood. John A. T. Robinson and Harvey Cox tell us not to believe in a "God out there," it being a biblical idea outdated in our modern world. Even Evangelical theologians want to talk about God as our ever-present companion.

But I wish to counter these ideas and say very strongly this morning: "Yes, there is a God out there." He is above us, beyond us, and sometimes very distant from us. The Bible, as we said earlier, affirms a God both near and far. God says, "Do I not fill heaven and earth?" Only this grand view of God can properly serve us in whatever situation we find ourselves; only this grand view of God can comfort people like myself when someone dear is taken away.

There is an old song we don't sing anymore building on 1 Cor 13:12, where Paul talks about seeing now in a mirror dimly, but one day seeing Christ "face to face." It goes:

> Face to face with Christ my savior
> Face to face—what will it be?
> When in rapture I behold Him
> Jesus Christ who died for me
>
> Face to face I shall behold Him
> Far beyond the starry sky
> Face to face in all His glory
> I shall see Him by and by.
> (Mrs. Frank A. Breck)

Yes, the day will come when we see that distant heaven where Jesus shines in all his glory, and shining with him will be Norm Larson, Ruth Lombard, Anna Hallberg, Joan Lundbom, and others whose presence we now miss. Our God fills heaven and earth. He is a God at hand and a God far off. AMEN

7

Something of Oneself, Something of Another[1]

Christmas

Text: John 3:16

For God so loved the world that he gave his only Son, so that everyone who believes in him may not perish but have eternal life.

TONIGHT MANY OF US will open gifts around the Christmas tree; for some it will be tomorrow morning on Christmas Day. The exchange of gifts is an ancient practice among Christians, rooted in the first-century-AD tradition of the wise men visiting Jesus with gifts of gold, frankincense, and myrrh. For many the buying of gifts has become the focal point of the celebration, and not a little has been said about the commercialization of Christmas. We are all a bit embarrassed, or should be, about the annual December "buyout." Yet giving is so basic to Christmas we cannot be without it.

Besides the story Matthew gives us of the wise men is a verse in John's Gospel giving an even better basis for Christmas giving. It is a verse we know by heart, one which speaks about our giving God. It begins: "For God so loved the world that he *gave* his only son . . ." We give gifts because God gave us a most precious gift. Our gifts proceed out of this joy.

---

1. Preached at the Covenant Church in Hopkinton, Massachusetts, on December 24, 1981.

But how do we give? And how successful are we in giving to others? We choose gifts in different ways, and the gifts we give must be measured not simply by how they are chosen, but by how they are received. A successful gift is a gift gratefully received.

Many of us, when we select gifts, choose something that appeals to us. It is natural to do so. There is, after all, something to be said for the man who buys a gift for another that when he gets home he wishes he could keep it for himself. Or there is the gift a woman chooses because she has one of her own, and likes it so much she wants someone else to have it. Gifts, then, can be giving something of yourself: the book you have read and enjoyed; your best loaf of bread or homemade jelly, your peanut brittle or spritz cookies; that item of stained glass you made, that carving out of wood, that hand-knitted sweater, that work done in needlepoint where even the design was your choice. It is fun to give away such gifts: They are tried, and more important something of yourself goes with the gift.

Yet gifts chosen because you like them do not always find their mark. People are different. What you like is not necessarily what someone else will like, or what someone else will think is best. Your favorite book may strike someone else as superficial reading, or as "too hard going"; your father may not appreciate a Charlie Brown calendar, even though you do, and you thought he would like it; even your best fruitcake will fall short of the mark if Aunt Betty does not like fruitcake, but says when you gave it that she liked the pretty tin it came in. Many gifts fail or, if they do not fail, they do not succeed as hoped because the likes and dislikes of the receiver were not taken into account.

Because of this we have been taught in recent years, by psychologists primarily, to be "other-centered" in our giving. The gifts we buy should be chosen not because we like them, but because we believe they will be liked by the person on the receiving end. The questions we should therefore ask before shopping or setting to work on a creation of our own are, "What kind of cookies does he like?" "What sort of sweater would she pick out for herself?" If Mom and Dad are coming for dinner, "Do they like fondue?" "Would my college-age daughter really like a year's subscription to *Reader's Digest*?" "Does Uncle Pete like to play games?" Gifts chosen with the other person in mind will hit the mark more than gifts chosen with oneself in mind. They require prior thought, maybe even some detective work. And the person you give them to knows you had them in mind, not someone else.

Something of Oneself, Something of Another

About the only way such a gift can fail is if you give something you know the other person will like, but you yourself do not like. Even if someone is made happy with your gift, you are left feeling empty because nothing of yourself went with it. And if the receiver discovers you do not like the gift, it can have an adverse effect. I confess to having given away wedding gifts my wife and I didn't want to keep—some milk-glass bowls, for example, that friends would probably like. People in business who do not drink Royal Gate Vodka will nevertheless give bottles of the spirit to friends at Christmas knowing that they are sure to like it. Parents give children gifts they know the children will like, but which they wholly or partially disapprove of. These gifts leave you feeling a bit empty. They may even leave you feeling guilty if you have given what is really not in your heart to give.

There is, however, another formula for gift-giving. It is one that will never fail, and never leave you feeling empty or guilty. Instead it will bind you and the person to whom you give the gift in a wonderful way. The formula is simple: You give a gift that has both yourself and the other person in mind. It is a gift you like, even one you treasure, and the other person will be known to like, perhaps also treasure. Such gifts are the most precious because they have a binding quality. Something of yourself goes into that something of another. Such gifts accent what you and another person have in common, a shared segment of life and the world bonding you in a relationship that is meaningful and lasting.

I recall the gift of a book on Vermont given to my wife and myself by the dean of Andover Newton Theological School some years ago. It was his favorite book on Vermont. We had just taken a trip to Vermont and come back excited about the sugaring houses, country stores, and adventures we had. He knew we loved Vermont. This gift had a wonderful binding quality. He liked the gift he was giving. And it was a gift he knew we would like.

Recently when we went to California, Linda decided to give her sister three coffee cups and saucers that were familiar items in the family home. Lois had also received cups and saucers years back when the family treasures were divided up, but they were destroyed in the earthquake of 1989. Linda knew Lois would treasure them, and because they were special to her, it turned out to be the perfect gift.

This year I got two wonderful jars of Swedish sill[2] from a friend who liked sill and had discovered that it was a favorite of mine. Another perfect gift—one that hit the mark and bound two sill lovers together. How glad I

---

2. Swedish sill is pickled herring.

am that my friend did not give me lutfisk![3] Gifts of this kind are not often given; in fact they are rare. But when they come—whether they be a homemade loaf of bread, a box of candy, a family portrait, a favorite game—they are the gifts most appreciated and most likely not to be forgotten. They create a bond between the giver and the receiver, which is more precious than the gift itself.

Which brings us back to John 3:16, which announces a gift of this last kind because it is something of God and something of us. The babe in the manger is at once a human child and the God of all creation: the two mysterious natures of Christ forming the discussion of the Fourth Ecumenical Council at Chalcedon in AD 451. This great gift—if we accept it—cannot possibly fail. In the baby of Bethlehem God emptied himself, but was not left empty. Jesus has bound us inextricably to God, yes, he has also reconciled us to himself, bringing peace to us and to the world. "Thanks be to God," says Paul, "for his indescribable gift" (2 Cor 9:15). AMEN

---

3. Aged stockfish pickled in lye, another Swedish delight for some.

Understanding the Christian Walk

8

The Sermon on the Mount[1]

Text: Matthew 7:24–27

Everyone then who hears these words of mine and acts on them will be like a wise man who built his house on rock. The rain fell, the floods came, and the winds blew and beat on that house, but it did not fall, because it had been founded on rock. And everyone who hears these words of mine and does not act on them will be like a foolish man who built his house on sand. The rain fell, and the floods came, and the winds blew and beat against that house, and it fell—and great was its fall!

Mbote! Greetings to all of you from Sigurd Westburg, Arden Almquist, Richard Anderson, and Robert Thornbloom.

The Sermon on the Mount is a collection of Jesus' greatest teachings. He goes up on a mountain with his disciples and says:

The poor and weak will be blessed

The righteous and pure in heart will see God

Those who suffer because they follow him will be blessed

Followers must be better people than the best Jews and the best Gentiles

One must not provoke another with inflammatory language

---

1. Preached on a "Big Sunday" at the Communauté Evangélique de l'Ubangi-Mongala Church in Bokada Ngambe, Zaire [Congo], on August 1, 1981. Translated by the Reverend Marvin Wickstrom into Lingala.

- One must not steal another's wife for himself
- One must bear insult, take a slap on the cheek, and not retaliate
- One must love one's enemies
- One must not pray or give alms to show how good one is
- One must seek first God and his rule, not clothes or food (to which we might add radios and other nice things)
- One must not judge others more harshly than judging oneself
- One must not be afraid to ask God for what one needs or wants.

This is a collection of great teachings, and the Bible says people liked to hear them. But Jesus is a good teacher not only because he gives teachings better than those of other teachers. He is a good teacher because he expects people to do what he teaches them. That is why at the end of the Sermon on the Mount he tells the story of the two houses. The wise man who builds his house on rock is the man Jesus wants, a man who hears his words and does them! It is not enough just to listen to Jesus, or to clap your hands at his wonderful words. You must obey.

Moses is the great teacher of the Old Testament. We can read some of his teachings to Israel in the book of Deuteronomy. People wondered if they could do them; perhaps they were too difficult. But listen to what Moses says:

> Surely, this commandment that I am commanding you today is not too hard for you, nor is it too far away. It is not in heaven, that you should say, "Who will go up to heaven for us, and get it for us so that we may hear it and observe it?" Neither is it beyond the sea, that you should say, "Who will cross to the other side of the sea for us, and get it for us so that we may hear it and observe it?" No, the word is very near to you; it is in your mouth and in your heart for you to observe. (Deut 30:11–14)

Moses was a great teacher because he expected people to do what he taught them.

Do you not think that those who teach your children in school will expect them to do what they are told? Will it help if your child brings the teacher an egg, pineapple, or makemba and then does not do his lesson? And what about you? If you bring your pastor a gift of food and do not do what he has taught you, will he be pleased?

The Sermon on the Mount

Neither will God be pleased if you read your Bible, pray loudly or softly, bring offerings to church, or come to Big Sunday and sing with the many who are gathered, and do not obey his commands. The Bible says that obedience is more important than sacrifice (1 Sam 15:22). If your house is to stand up in the storm, you must obey Jesus.

Do not be afraid that it will be too difficult. You can do it! Moses told the Israelites that they could do it. Jesus, too, is not a hard master. His teachings are easy. Hear what he says:

> Come to me, all you that are weary and are carrying heavy burdens, and I will give you rest. Take my yoke upon you, and learn from me; for I am gentle and humble in heart, and you will find rest for your souls. For my yoke is easy, and my burden is light. (Matt 11:28–30)

9

"My Yoke Is Easy and My Burden Is Light"[1]

Text: Matthew 11:28–30

Come to me, all you that are weary and carrying heavy burdens, and I will give you rest. Take my yoke upon you, and learn from me; for I am gentle and humble in heart, and you will find rest for your souls. For my yoke is easy, and my burden is light.

Ich bin dankbar Heute Morgen für die Einladung in ihre Gemeinde zu predigen. Leider, muß Ich auf English predigen. Aber, Ich habe in Ernie Engelbert ein guten Übersetzer, und er wird mir helfen. Er gesagt hat, er kann mich mit Einfühlungs-vermögen übersetzen. Vielleicht ist sein Predigt besser als meine. Aber Gottes Wort ist besser und klarer als die Worte von Ernie und mir. Nun möchte Ich den Predigt Text von Heute Lesen, er steht in Matt 11:28–30.

In recent days we have heard loud cries for freedom in our world: People in the Baltic states of Estonia, Latvia, and Lithuania want more freedom. In Russia, Armenia, and other parts of the old Soviet Union people are clamoring for political and economic freedom. We have heard the cries in Poland, Hungary, and the other states of Eastern Europe, which for forty years have languished under communist rule. Since a month ago six thousand people have fled the DDR in a circuitous route through Hungary. More will likely

---

1. Preached at the Freie evangelische Gemeinde, Marburg, Germany, on June 11, 1989. Translated by Dr. Ernie Engelbert into German.

"My Yoke Is Easy and My Burden Is Light"

follow. Then a week ago, on June 11, protests that began two months earlier in Beijing's Tiananmen Square were silenced by gunfire. My neighbor from Mainland China presently at the university is trying to help me understand what is going on in her country.

In Bosnia-Herzegovina Muslims want freedom from Christian Serbs, while Christians in southern Sudan for many years have sought freedom from Muslims in the north if only someone would hear their cries. In another month the attention of the world will focused on France, which will celebrate its bicentennial of the French Revolution. In America the bicentennial of our revolution was celebrated a little over a decade ago. The most precious freedoms won in our revolution were for human rights. Those standing over against freedom fighters—in all places and in all ages—are guardians of law and order. With them power and authority rests.

Here in Europe battles for freedom were fought over 450 years ago at the time of the Renaissance, which unleashed the enormous creativity leading to the Protestant Reformation. At the time power and authority rested largely in Rome, home of the Western Church. Luther was the great apostle of freedom. After reading Paul's Letter to the Romans, Luther began writing and preaching about freedom in Christ. His entire life was in revolt against a church weighted down with too much law, too much doctrine, and too little grace.

Calvin, too, wanted to shake off heavy burdens imposed by the church, but he did not free it from law and doctrine. When it came to both, he merely substituted one set for another. Calvin studied law in Paris until he was twenty-four, and the result was a legacy of legalism in Reformed Churches that is still with us today. Linda and I visited Geneva about three weeks ago and saw there the stern face of Calvin cut into even sterner stone.

Calvin ruled Geneva with an iron hand. Listen to some of the cases brought before him and the Consistory:

Herr Baumann has not attended church in a month;

Frau Petermann has been heard gossiping;

One person was caught sleeping in church;

One fellow had written "nonsense" over Calvin's writings;

Someone had eaten fish on Good Friday (which was forbidden);

One person claimed there was no devil and no hell;

One person was overheard praising the pope; and

Another betrothed his daughter to a Catholic.

These individuals were brought before the Consistory, and if the charges were found to be true, they were punished. Records in Geneva tell us that one man was punished for three days simply because he laughed during a sermon. Take heed! Small wonder people opposing Calvin in Geneva called themselves "Libertines," i.e., people wanting freedom.

The situation in Puritan New England was not much different. There, too, the influence of Calvin was felt in a legalistic brand of Christianity. Freedom movements in America have been in reaction to this for decades, a reaction that continues to this very day.

Now the Bible, of course, contains law, multiple codes of law, at the center of which lies the Ten Commandments. It also has something to say about freedom, although not as much as you might think. Freedom is not an important Old Testament theme. Paul will later talk about freedom when contrasting freedom achieved in Christ with bondage imposed by Jewish law (Gal 5:1–14). The Pharisees had 613 laws which they took to be binding on people—an oppressive number!

The key idea in both the Old Testament and New Testament is embodied in the Hebrew words ישועה / ישע, which we translate as "salvation," "deliverance," or "liberation." They appear in the proper names Joshua and Jesus, the latter being the Greek form of Joshua. There are two major acts of liberation in the Bible among a number of lesser ones: (1) In the Old Testament the great act of liberation is Israel's liberation from slavery in Egypt; and (2) In the New Testament the great act of liberation is Jesus' death on the cross, a liberation from sin for all people of the world (John 3:16).

Liberation, however, is not to be simply equated with freedom. It is a release, but not in the sense we usually think freedom to be. Liberation in the Bible is a change of masters. In the Old Testament the old master is the pharaoh of Egypt, the new master the Lord God. In the New Testament the old master is Satan and the power of sin, the new master Jesus the Christ.

In the Old Testament the model for this powerful idea emanates from ancient Near Eastern law. In the ancient world where people fell into slavery, they could, under certain conditions, be redeemed by a family member or next of kin. That person paid the price of redemption—which the enslaved person could not pay—and the slave, when freed, was put under his charge. The person was not entirely free. He or she had a new master, who was the redeeming kin. And with the redemption came new obligations. But here is the good news: Because the new master was a relative, the servitude was more benevolent than before. It would be like getting a no-interest loan

"My Yoke Is Easy and My Burden Is Light"

from your parents or your uncle, which is better than a loan from Dresdner Bank under the best of terms.

In Exodus 20:2 the Lord says to Israel at Mount Sinai: "I am the Lord your God, who brought you out of the land of Egypt, out of the house of slavery, (therefore)..." What follows are the Ten Commandments. Pharaoh was the old oppressive master; the new benevolent master will be the Lord. In Exodus 4:22 the Lord calls Israel his "firstborn son," another indication that he is acting like someone on behalf of a member in the family.

The law consisted of new demands placed by Israel's new master, not meant to be the oppressive burden it later became. It was, for example, much less severe than common law seeking revenge at a 7-to-1 (or 77-to-1) ratio (Gen 4:23–24). It was the Lord's design to put Israel under an easy yoke; the Lord expected Israel to do the law without difficulty. Moses tells the people in Moab:

> Surely, this commandment that I am commanding you today is not too hard for you, nor is it too far away. It is not in heaven, that you should say, "Who will go up to heaven for us, and get it for us so that we may hear it and observe it?" Neither is it beyond the sea, that you should say, "Who will cross to the other side of the sea for us, and get it for us so that we may hear it and observe it?" No, the word is very near to you; it is in your mouth and in your heart for you to observe. (Deut 30:11–14)

Things are essentially no different in the New Testament, where Jesus, the new master, liberates, saves, or redeems all people from sin and their old master, the devil. Jesus' demands appear in the Sermon on the Mount where they are not meant to be oppressive. That he expects people to be able to do his commands is clear from the parable of the two houses given at the end. Jesus says,

> Everyone then who hears these words of mine and acts on them will be like a wise man who built his house on rock. The rain fell, the floods came, and the winds blew and beat on that house, but it did not fall, because it had been founded on rock. And everyone who hears these words of mine and does not act on them will be like a foolish man who built his house on sand. The rain fell, and the floods came, and the winds blew and beat against that house, and it fell—and great was its fall! (Matt 7:24–27)

Jesus is addressing a people overburdened with too much law and tired of endless debate among the rabbis over doctrine. Many were mentally weary and distressed. Jesus addresses a people who need rest, and to them he says the words of our text:

> Come to me, all you that are weary and are carrying heavy burdens, and I will give you rest. Take my yoke upon you, and learn from me; for I am gentle and humble in heart, and you will find rest for your souls. For my yoke is easy, and my burden is light.

What can we learn from this scripture? First of all, we must know that Jesus is our master and all stand under his lordship. Second, as followers of Jesus we are not entirely free. Paul says, "Do you not know that . . . you are not your own? For you were bought with a price" (1 Cor 6:19–20). How important to know that we are owned by a benevolent master and beholden to him. How important to read the Bible and study it. It is not enough to be able to quote a verse from here or there. One must read the whole Bible, which takes time and work. If we begin with the Sermon on the Mount, we learn that we are not free. We are not free to be provocative and insulting in our language; not free to commit adultery or wanting to commit adultery; not free to swear falsely or speak recklessly; not free to seek revenge if someone insults us. But we are free to love our enemies! We are free to emulate a God who wants us to be like him.

Finally, we must know that Jesus' yoke is easy and his burden light. Not with all sorts of ironclad rules, many of which are not of ultimate importance, are we to make the yoke difficult and the burden heavy. May the Lord deliver us from people more demanding than God himself. If you feel today that the Christian walk is too difficult and too burdensome, something is wrong. Jesus did not intend it be so. Discipleship was not intended to be so difficult that people could not attempt it. He said: "For my yoke is easy, and my burden is light." AMEN

10

Invitation to Adventure[1]

Lent

Text: John 14:1-6

"Do not let your hearts be troubled. Believe in God, believe also in me. In my Father's house there are many dwelling places. If it were not so, would I have told you that I go to prepare a place for you? And if I go and prepare a place for you, I will come again and will take you to myself, so that where I am, there you may be also. And you know the way to the place where I am going." Thomas said to him, "Lord, we do not know where you are going. How can we know the way?" Jesus said to him, "I am the way, and the truth, and the life. No one comes to the Father except through me."

Paul Tournier, the Swiss psychiatrist who combines clinical observations so successfully with Christian faith, has written a book titled *The Adventure of Living*. It has one basic thesis, which is that "life can and should be an adventure." Tournier says individual lives need adventure; married couples and families need adventure; and societies, too, must allow opportunities for adventure—something lacking in many countries of our world where rigid social and political ideologies reign. Above all, says Tournier, the Christian life should be an adventure. It should be the ultimate adventure.

1. Preached at the Covenant Church in Hilmar, California, on February 18, 1979.

After all, God himself is shown to be adventurous, beginning at creation where Tournier sees the creation of man and woman to be a bold and daring act.

What is an adventure? We think instinctively of journeys, e.g., trips, vacations, bike rides across America, and the like. But other adventures can occur right at home: writing a poem; drawing a picture, sewing a dress, making a model airplane; eating popcorn on the couch with someone special; taking on a project in your backyard; repairing your car, your bicycle, a room in your house; preparing food from a recipe for the first time; rolling on the floor with your child.

Tournier says carnivals bring out our thirst for adventure. So do sports and the reading of books. When children play sports and do other things, parents—also grandparents—can join in and live the adventure with them. I think for anything to be an adventure it must contain the following:

(1) There must be some excitement; there has to be passion involved, a bit of humor perhaps, something unusual or out of the ordinary that makes your blood run faster.

(2) Adventures must contain some peril or risk. There has to be a possibility of failure, disappointment, even loss: your poem or picture may not turn out well; your new recipe could flop; a dress could be ruined; you may not succeed away at college; your trip could end up a disaster; even eating popcorn with that special someone could a disappointment. But for an adventure to be a true adventure perils have to be overcome. If they are not, you no longer have an adventure, but tragedy.

(3) Perhaps the most important feature of an adventure is that the outcome, to some extent, has to be uncertain. If you take a trip and know the road well, knowing precisely where you will end up and experiencing nothing unusual en route, it is unlikely you will have an adventure. A smooth trip is one for which we are always grateful, but it probably will not be an adventure. Great stories emanate from trips where problems were encountered. Likewise, jobs routine in nature carry little or no adventure.

My grandfather had a spirit of adventure and I remember as a boy listening eagerly to his stories. He traveled alone from his home in Kewanee, Illinois, to Chicago to attend the World's Fair in 1893. Then as a young man he left Kewanee for Texas with an older brother who had tuberculosis,

Invitation to Adventure

hoping that drier climate would help cure this dreaded illness. Sister Winnie came along to keep house, but she became lonely in this desolate area of western Texas and returned home. Eventually, Grandpa and Winfrid moved to Colorado Springs, which also had a less humid climate, and there he met my grandmother, who had embarked on an adventure of her own with two older brothers, leaving Boone, Iowa, to find work and excitement in Denver.

After getting married, my grandparents settled in Chicago. But grandpa's thirst for adventure remained very much alive. In 1923 he drove with a friend to see a beautiful lake three hundred miles north of Chicago called Spread Eagle. It was in Wisconsin, just across the Menominee River from Iron Mountain, Michigan. He was smitten with the place, and promptly bought a lot, returning the next year to build a cottage with help from friends who came with him. The day came when he was ready to take the family to Spread Eagle. He had told my grandmother, my mother and her two sisters, what a wonderful place to expect in the most beautiful place on God's earth. He had everything prepared and could hardly wait for them to see it.

The trip north to Spread Eagle in those days was long and difficult—nine or ten hours, flat tires, often other car problems, detours, and gravel roads north of Green Bay. I remember hearing about the first family trip. Anticipation had peaked. The story is that my grandmother, when she first saw the place sat down in the woods and cried, "Otto, how could you have brought us to such a desolate place?" My grandfather was hurt. Yet within a short time her attitude turned a full 180 degrees. She came to love the place, and spent her last days there in the summer of 1957.

According to Tournier, shared adventures are the most exciting. I carried on the tradition of my grandfather. Linda and I, just after we were married, left for a year of study, travel, and for her an anticipated job teaching school in Beirut. Departing Germany in a Volkswagen, we began the three-thousand-mile drive to a place we had never seen. Triple A could supply with only some roadmaps; much of the journey was uncharted. This shared trip ended up being a series of adventures. We blew a tire in Yugoslavia and could not get it repaired until arriving in Greece. One night we had to sleep in the car, in a cornfield off the road, in the rain, because a room could not be had in Belgrade. We drank a strange-tasting Yugo-Cola for two days, and ate Wiener schnitzel every breakfast, lunch, and dinner because "Wiener schnitzel" was the one food we could pronounce that they could understand. On our final morning in the Austro-German region I simply took the waiter by the arm, marched with him into the kitchen, and pointed to food we could eat. We had good eggs that morning. We explored a medieval castle that was visible from the road, ascending a winding road and waving to an old man and children riding in wooden-wheeled wagon.

In Istanbul we had to drive at night with our headlights off, with other motorists honking loudly if we turned them on. Why? I still do not know. In Ankara we were delayed a day when the Syrian embassy refused to issue us a transit visa through Syria, but then the next day, after some interrogation, they did issue us one. We nearly got stoned by Syrian shepherd boys, who, at first were friendly when we asked to take their picture, but then became hostile when we did not toss them enough coins. When arriving in Beirut we were taken in by a pastor and his wife until we could find an apartment, which proved difficult. Then we had to wait some anxious days to see if Linda would get a teaching job at the American Community School. Had this not worked out, we would have had to return home in a couple months. One teacher failed to show up and Linda got the job.

This was not an odyssey just for fun. I was in seminary preparing for the ministry, and our reason for going to Beirut was for me to study a year at the Near East School of Theology and the American University of Beirut, also to visit Jerusalem and other places in the Holy Land. We had prayed that God would bless our undertaking; we believed fully that we ought to be going; we had made every conceivable preparation before leaving home. Still, we did not know how every detail would work out. Linda would know for certain about her job only after we were on location. We have had other shared adventures since, many of them, each with its own excitement, risk, and uncertain outcome.

Adventures with uncertain outcomes, however, can end up being great disappointments. There was a popular song recorded by Tammy Wynette some years ago in which she sang about how she and her man went from place to place, even "up north to Alaska," but, "they didn't find it there, so [they] moved on." She ended with the words, "I know you're tired of following my elusive dreams and schemes . . . they're only fleeting things."

People today, in countless ways, are desperately looking for adventure and not finding it: drugs end up being a "bad trip"; lotteries and gamblings end up in loss, sometimes huge loss; illicit sexual romps and other types of reckless living end in guilt and remorse—all adventures that turn out not to be adventures.

Invitation to Adventure

Which brings us back to the Christian walk. Is it an adventure? Do people in the Bible live lives of adventure in their walk of faith? Stories about Abraham, Jacob, and Joseph would lead us to believe that adventure with God is possible, maybe even the norm. So also stories about Ruth and Esther. And what about the exodus from Egypt? Was not this a grand adventure for Israel?

In the Old Testament (2 Sam 15:19–22) we meet up too with Ittai the Gittite, a non-Israelite man who came to David the day before the king was making hurried plans to leave Jerusalem to flee Absalom, his son who was bent on taking the kingdom from him. Ittai offers to go with David and his entourage, wherever the journey takes them. There will be risk and uncertainty. David may never return to Jerusalem, so he advises the man to go home. But Ittai wants to remain with him. Is he showing loyalty as some other Israelites are? Maybe. But he is a foreigner. It could also be that Ittai is simply willing to embark on an adventure. We don't know.

In John 14 things are more clear, but they are reversed. Jesus is challenging his disciples to embark on an adventure, and they are not sure they want to go. Thomas says, "Lord, we do not know where you are going; how can we know the way?" (v. 5). Well, you say, Thomas is the doubter. Yes, but his question may also be the question of the others; it is frequently the question of people today. This mansion with many dwelling places (v. 2) is hidden from us and the way is also hidden. One must follow Jesus, who is the way, the truth, and the life. Sounds like an invitation to adventure.

According to Tournier, Jesus had earlier called his disciples to embark on an adventure, and very quickly they left fishing nets, tax tables, and other stations to follow him. What is happening now? Have these same individuals lost their sense of adventure now that Jesus is about to leave them? Perhaps youth invites adventure more readily than old age. Also, new arrivals may be more adventurous than those who have been around a long time. Ittai was a newcomer. The disciples, too, when newcomers, were more adventurous in following Jesus than they are now at the seeming end of Jesus' ministry.

It has often been noted that new people coming into the church tend to be more adventurous than those who have been around a long time. It is not always so, but the phenomenon is real. You and I know Christians who can only sing, "I shall, I shall, I shall not be moved." Tournier says that any sincere conversion draws the convert into a great spiritual adventure. It can be a first-time conversion, or a renewal of faith after a prolonged period of stagnation.

How is your life with God and with Jesus Christ? Would you call it an adventure? Does it have excitement? Do you live this day with a passion? Do you welcome the new and the unusual, looking to see how both can fit together for good? Are you able to meet peril with confidence, uncertainty with resolve, and accept risk with hope? Or does the unknown frighten you? Boredom is a serious malady—in marriages, in family life, in society, in the church. Something is awry if you become bored with your spouse, bored with your children, bored with your job, and bored with Christ and his church.

Life is to be an adventure, with life following Jesus Christ the ultimate adventure. Jesus has gone to prepare a place for us. It will be a wonderful place—better than Spread Eagle, an unvisited camping site, or some other place we have never seen. He is coming to get us and take us there. We do not know precisely where this place is, but we follow the one who does—this Jesus, who says, "I am the way, the truth, and the life; no one comes to the Father but by me." AMEN

11

"What Is That to You? Follow Me!"[1]

Easter

Text: John 21:20–22

Peter turned and saw the disciple whom Jesus loved following them; he was the one who had reclined next to Jesus and the supper and had said, "Lord, who is it that is going to betray you?" When Peter saw him, he said to Jesus, "Lord, what about him?" Jesus said to him, "If it is my will that he remain until I come, what is that to you? Follow me!"

In the Gospel of John the last person to speak with Jesus is Peter. The disciples have just had breakfast with the risen Jesus on the beach and Jesus has an outstanding account to settle with the impetuous fisherman. The relationship is broken because Peter at the trial denied knowing him. Jesus asks Peter, "Simon, son of John, do you love me more than these?" Peter says he does. Jesus says, "Feed my lambs." Jesus asks the question again. Peter repeats his answer, "Yes Lord, you know that I love you." Jesus says, "Tend my sheep." Jesus asks the question a third time, and Peter becomes angry, saying, "Lord, you know everything; you know that I love you." Jesus says, "Feed my sheep." We who look on know what is happening. We

---

1. Preached in the chapel of the Lutheran Theological Seminary, Hong Kong, on September 21, 2010. Simultaneous translations provided into Cantonese and Mandarin.

remember Peter's three denials and see now that Jesus is asking for three affirmations of love. After Peter's vigorous affirmation, Jesus continues:

> Very truly, I tell you, when you were younger, you used to fasten your own belt and go wherever you wished. But when you grow old, you will stretch out your hands, and someone else will fasten a belt around you and take you where you do not wish to go. (John 21:18)

John adds that this was to indicate the kind of death by which Peter would glorify God. Jesus says in conclusion, "Follow me!" (John 21:19).

In Jesus' words is another echo out of the past. Peter may remember that it was on these same shores of the Sea of Galilee, when he and Andrew were throwing their nets into the water, that Jesus appeared one day and said, "Follow me, and I will make you fishers of men." And they dropped their nets and followed him. Jesus was a young rabbi and to be one of his disciples was an excitement Peter could still remember. He and Andrew were not disappointed—those teachings opening up the Scriptures, those miracles, those adoring crowds of people on the hillside.

Oh, to follow then was pure joy. Now, however, the words "Follow me" are more difficult to hear. The journey ahead will include suffering and death. Peter gives no enthusiastic response. In fact, he wants to know if suffering will be the lot of everyone who follows Jesus. He turns to the beloved disciple, thought by many to be John, and says: "Lord, what about this man?" (John 21:21). Jesus answers: "If it is my will that he remain until I come, what is that to you? Follow me!" (v. 22). No word about the beloved disciple being lifted up with his belt and carried to a place he does not wish to go—a word Peter may have been waiting for. Nothing said about suffering. Nothing said about death. Sounds a bit unfair, doesn't it? Jesus says only, "What is that to you? Follow me!"

There are lessons to be learned from this passage, and I wish to lift up three for our thinking this morning. The first is this: Sometimes it becomes necessary to balance off earlier denials with later affirmations, which may not be easy. Like Peter, we may become angry if we have to do it.

Shimei, son of Gera, met David and his entourage when they were evacuating Jerusalem at the time Absalom was making his bid to become king. At the sight of David, Shemei unleashed a string of curses and threw at the king handfuls of stones.

"What Is That to You? Follow Me!"

> Out! Out! Murderer! Scoundrel!" The Lord has avenged on all of you the blood of the house of Saul, in whose place you have reigned; and the Lord has given the kingdom into the hand of your son Absalom. See, disaster has overtaken you; for you are a man of blood. (2 Sam 16:7–8)

David took the abuse, although those with him wanted to cut off Shimei's head. Even as they walked away, Shimei continued his cursing, throwing more stones, and tossing handfuls of dust at David for good measure.

But after the rebellion was over and David was on his way back to Jerusalem, who should come running to meet David at the Jordan? Why, it was Shimei, and with him one thousand Benjaminites. Shimei fell at David's feet, asking the king not to remember what he said the day David left Jerusalem. Yes, he sinned by cursing the Lord's anointed, but now he wants to be among the first to meet the king on his return. Some are still calling for Shemei's head. But David says "No!" Nothing will mar the day's celebration. Shimei will live, not die. He balanced off his former curses with later affirmations (2 Sam 19:16–23).

People today are sometimes required to make similar reversals. They find three or more things wrong with the church before discovering three or more things right about it; they state why they cannot make a commitment to Christ before they come up with a good reason why they should make a commitment; or they give multiple reasons why they cannot give generously to God's work only to come around later to discovering how good it feels to be generous.

Perhaps you have compromised your commitment to Jesus by acting wrongly toward another person, in which case Jesus may be asking you today to balance off earlier words of censure with words of repentance and affirmation. It's not enough to say, "I didn't mean it." Perhaps you didn't. It may not be enough to say, "I couldn't help it." Maybe you couldn't. It may not even be enough to say, "It won't happen again." Others are saying, "It better not!"

What is needed is a positive statement, one without ambiguity. Shimei said, "I have sinned." Peter said, "I love you; you know that I love you." You might try saying, "I was wrong." A confession cleaning out a muddied soul and contrite words are what give real peace and have the best chance in bringing about reconciliation, if such be needed. Judges give maximum penalties to those who showing no remorse for their wrongdoing. Let us not imagine that God will act any differently toward people who refuse to repent.

Second, we learn from our text that while God's call can be accepted with relative ease, renewing it may occur only with great courage. Abraham's call in Genesis 12 was one of the greatest calls ever issued by God: to make of this man a great nation, to bless him, to make his name great, and through him to bless all people of the earth. God's promise was unconditional, unilateral, and eternal. But it was another matter when God told Abraham to bind his son, his only son, and sacrifice him on an altar. Was there no hurt here? Was there no testing of faith? Isaac was as good as dead when deliverance came. No, following God turned out to be no bed of roses for Abraham. The decision earlier to follow God was renewed only with great courage.

Prophets, too, although they may have received God's call with relative ease, would later discover that the going was tough. Isaiah had his wondrous vision in the temple, only to take early retirement when Ahaz paid him no heed, and having to reenter public life later when Hezekiah became king.

Jeremiah was not overly joyful when the call came to be God's prophet (Jer 1:4–12), but there was joy when words promised for his mouth actually came. He reflected later:

> Your words were found and I ate them
> > and your word was to me for joy
> > and for the gladness of my heart
> For your name is called upon me
> > Yahweh, the God of Hosts.
> I sat not in the happy crowd and acted jolly
> > because of your hand, all alone I sat
> > for with indignation you filled me.
> (Jer 15:16–17 AB)

But now he is older, having had some years in the Lord's employ, and the tone of his voice changes. He has known suffering, much suffering, and cries out:

> Why has my pain become continual
> > and my blow desperate
> > refusing to be healed?
> Will you really be for me as a deceptive stream
> > waters that are not sure?
> (Jer 15:18 AB)

"What Is That to You? Follow Me!"

Ezekiel found that after his thrilling vision of God's glory and having eaten a scroll said to be "sweet as honey" in his mouth (Ezek 3:3), its words when digested became so bitter that he went away in the heat of his spirit and sat speechless before the exiles on Tel-abib's riverbank seven days (Ezek 3:14–15).

Not many of us are called to walk the road Abraham walked, nor are many tested in their faith like the prophets, the apostle Peter, and others. But you and I know people, who, this very day are renewing their faith amidst suffering, real suffering. Some are looking death in the face. Others are experiencing a suffering they tell you is worse than death.

Thirdly, we learn from our text that following Jesus means that experiences coming to us will not necessarily come to those standing next to us, or vice versa. Peter was told that he would suffer a death like his master, and tradition tells us that he did—being crucified upside down, at his request. Apparently he got the message, and carried it a step further. But his lot was not to be the lot of the beloved disciple.

In times of difficulty, whether it be sickness, misfortune, or some other trouble, we are quick to ask with Peter, 'What about that man, Lord? What about that woman over there?' Jesus says: "What is that to you, Follow me!" Our eyes must remain on him, not the person next to us. He is the one to follow. It may mean suffering; it may mean a lot of suffering; but it may mean not much, or very little. Our lot will be different from the lot of those next to us even though we are sure to share trials with family members, friends, and others.

But we need not become imbittered if we have to endure a trial the person next to us is not asked to endure. Also, we need not feel guilty when spared sufferings other people must undergo, although we remain sensitive to those sufferings—enough to be compassionate and caring. We also need not become paralyzed when tragedy befalls someone dear to us, thinking the same will happen to us. I know people who become victimized at fifty-five because their mother died of cancer at fifty-five. I know people, who, because a brother developed arthritis, thought they too would be get arthritis. They might; they might not. I know parents who become fearful about leaving their child asleep at night because a close friend lost a child in a crib death. Yes, infirmities are hereditary, and calamities of one compare to calamities of others. But the point is that God gives each person their test, their suffering, and their grace in his own good measure.

Oil Enough to Make the Journey

The Christian walk is a call to follow Jesus. When comparisons are made to others, as they inevitably will be, Jesus' words remain to you and me what they were to Peter: "What is that to you? Follow me!" Learning this will broaden our faith. It will broaden the witness we give to others. Finally, these words might, surprisingly, be for us words of good news. AMEN.

12

Faith Seeks Understanding[1]

Text: Mark 9:30–32

They went on from there and passed through Galilee. He did not want anyone to know it; for he was teaching his disciples, saying to them, "The Son of Man is to betrayed into human hands, and they will kill him, and three days after being killed, he will rise again." But they did not understand what he was saying and were afraid to ask him.

I feel a closeness to all of you because of a deep friendship with Guro and Peder Liland, with whom my son David stayed this past year. I rejoice in the unity we have in Jesus Christ. Greetings from our churches in the United States.

In the Middle Ages a classic discussion took place between two great theologians of the church, Saint Thomas Aquinas and Saint Anselm. It had to do with the relation of faith and understanding. Aquinas said one needed to have understanding before one could have faith, faith being a sort of leap when one came to the point where understanding had reached its limit. Anselm said, no. In his view faith must come first; it must precede reflection and discussion of religious things. We do not learn and learn more so we can believe; we believe in order that we may arrive at a knowledge of what we believe. In other words, "faith seeks understanding."

They may both be right. Everyone, it would seem, needs understanding of at least an elementary sort to believe what the Bible teaches, who

---

1. Preached at the Tabernaklet Baptistkirke in Stavanger, Norway, on May 17, 1985. Translated by Dr. Peder Liland into Norwegian.

Jesus is, and what God's will is for the world. We know, too, that it is necessary to believe, to take what philosophers call that "leap of faith," to understand what one believes.

The church in large part has followed Anselm, coming to realize that knowledge, or understanding, will not lead us into penetrating and accepting the divine mysteries. To imagine that we only need to know more or understand more in order to believe in God, in Jesus Christ, in Jesus' death on the cross for the salvation of the world, will not take us where we need to go in our Christian walk.

But there are those, nevertheless, who think they need to read just one more book or hear just one more preacher or learn just one more great truth about the universe before they can really fall into the arms of God. But none leads them there. They only keep looking for more books, searching for more knowledge, talking to more people—the quest is endless.

Salvation, it would seem, comes in first believing. Then one can seek to understand what one believes. Sometimes understanding comes; sometimes one has to wait awhile before one understands; and sometimes one is never sure whether one really understands this or that about Christian belief. There are great mysteries of the faith never fully understood. All theologians recognize this, with "mystery" being appreciated more in the Eastern Church than in the Church of the West. Latin *sacramentum*, from which we get our word "sacrament," translates Greek *mystērion*.

Poor Job! Who can understand his suffering? His life as portrayed in the book bearing his name has captured the imagination of many, and greatly puzzled all. The eternal fascination with Job may lie in this very fact, namely, that we do not know why God permitted him to suffer. Job doesn't understand, and God's answer to him out of the whirlwind only shows that Job uttered what he did not understand (Job 42:3). God never answers the *why* question.

In the story preceding our scripture today, the father of that child who for years was unable to speak cries out even before the child is rid of the unclean spirit, "I believe; help my unbelief" (Mark 9:24). He does not say, "I believe, help me understand." Jesus simply told him to believe, and he did. The disciples have a problem, too, when Jesus goes on to tell them he will be betrayed, killed, and in three days rise again. Mark says, "But they did not understand what he was saying and were afraid to ask him." All through the Gospel of Mark we hear how the disciples are unable to understand. Yet they hang on. Is it because they believed?

Faith Seeks Understanding

I hear often very honest confessions of people when suffering or undergoing some sort of testing, say, "I do not understand this!" These are Christian people; people who have been a help to others; people who are brave; people who believe. Yet they do not understand. We must be careful not to confuse a failure to understand with disbelief. It may be that some plight has brought belief into question, but simply to say we do not know what is going on is not a loss of faith.

The fortieth anniversary of the end of World War II in Europe has once again brought to the world's attention the infamous Nazi rule in Germany, particularly its inhuman persecution of the Jews. In connection with this anniversary, our American president has been the subject of criticism because of his visit to the military cemetery in Bitburg, Germany, where many German soldiers are buried, some of them members of Hitler's Waffen-SS troops. I have been reading in the papers and listening to Jewish leaders speak about how there can never be forgiveness for the atrocities done during this time; they say there is no way to let the Holocaust die; it must be remembered forever.

I confess to being troubled by this. And I think the reason I am troubled, and the reason I support our president's visit to Bitburg, is that I believe forgiveness is ultimately a faith issue, not an issue requiring understanding. Faith must seek understanding; it cannot be the other way around. Other children besides Jewish children were killed by the Nazis. And were Russian, Polish, Norwegian, German, and other lives any less valuable than Jewish lives? Many non-Jews suffered in the concentration camps of Auschwitz and Buchenwald.

I can understand how someone might say, "I will never understand what happened." Inflicted suffering on such a grand scale is impossible to understand. It has happened in other wars; it is happening in our world today. I cannot understand how Jesus was so shamefully put to death. And even more difficult to understand is how this blatant injustice was to bring about reconciliation of God and people of our world (John 3:14–16).

We have been told by Jesus, who was a Jew, to forgive those who persecute us, pray for them, and live not with perpetual memories of evil but to rejoice when ill-treated because a reward awaits us in the kingdom of heaven. Paul, another Jew, told the Roman church, "Do not be overcome by evil, but overcome evil with good" (Rom 12:21).

We are like those disciples who could not understand some things— some very important things. Yet, if we are to go on living, if we are to be followers of Jesus Christ, we must believe in forgiveness, then seek to the best of our ability to try and understand. AMEN

13

Christians Neither Hot Nor Cold[1]

Worldwide Communion

Text: Revelation 3:15-17

I know your works; you are neither cold nor hot. I wish that you were either cold or hot. So, because you are lukewarm, and neither cold nor hot, I am about to spit you out of my mouth. For you say, "I am rich, I have prospered, and I need nothing." You do not realize that you are wretched, pitiable, poor, blind, and naked.

This message, spoken to the church at Laodicea, is the last of seven given to churches of Asia as they face a time of testing. Life in the Roman world was heating up, and many Christians were wondering whether they could meet the persecutions and challenges from a pagan religion. The message of Revelation comes through John, the divine seer, but the speaker is really the resurrected and glorified Christ, who addresses the seven churches from the heavenly throne around which stand messengers waiting to run with his message.

The messenger (or angel) to Laodicea is called. He is told to speak words of the Amen, the faithful and true witness, the beginning of God's creation. Who is this? It is Jesus, God's Word, as John told us at the beginning

---

1. Preached at the Covenant Church in Hilmar, California, on November 11, 1979.

of his Gospel, the Word made flesh (John 1:1–14). Jesus is the one sending the messenger to the Laodicean church.

Each of the churches has its own particular character, and the church at Laodicea is charged with lukewarmness. It is neither hot nor cold, and because of this it receives harsh judgment. Jesus finds lukewarmness so distasteful that he says he will spit these people out of his mouth. That is, if they do not repent from the state in which they are currently in.

Perhaps it is a surprise to you, as it is to me, that a young church in the first century AD could be in such a state. I usually think of early Christians as never flagging in zeal, aglow in the Spirit, and ever willing to serve the Lord. But here is a church apparently not so. Jesus identifies the problem: people in the church of Laodicea are suffering from self-sufficiency, success, and prosperity. Does this sound strange? Perhaps so, but contradictions of this nature abound—in our churches, in our communities, in our nation, and deep within the human soul. To overlook such contradictions is to miss what Scripture has to teach us about ourselves and the world we live in.

Here in Laodicea there is a contradiction in how the church perceives itself and how Jesus perceives it. The church says: "I am rich; I have prospered, and I need nothing." Jesus says: "You may not know it, but you are wretched, pitiable, poor, blind and naked." It is known that Laodicea was a prosperous city that took pride in its financial wealth, its commercial activities, and in having a medical center that was world-famous. Those last three words—*poor*, *blind*, and *naked*—were not randomly chosen. They are the exact opposites of being financially well-off, having exceptional medical facilities, and being an enviable clothier.

Laodicea was a banking center like Zurich, London, or New York. Cicero went there to cash large treasury bills. Following the earthquake of AD 60–61, Laodicea refused a government subsidy to rebuild the city because it was able to rebuild with its own resources. The Roman historian Tacitus records that other cities accepted aid again and again. Laodiceans were not what you would call poor.

Laodicea was also home to a famous medical center—like Rochester, Minnesota, home to Mayo Clinic. Ancient historical records (e.g., the Jewish Talmud) tell us that the famous Phrygian powder, an eye medication, originated here. How then could people of this city be called blind? They were justly famous for helping to restore people's sight.

Laodicea was also a center for the manufacture of woolens and carpets from native black wool, which originated in the area. Here we might compare the city to Pendleton, Oregon, or Fall River, Massachusetts. People here were certainly not naked. Most likely they were well-dressed.

We are impressed today if our cities or our country as a whole can boast such qualities: We are proud that our corn and wheat feed the world; we are proud that foreign leaders come to our hospitals for surgery or to get medical treatment; we are proud that our stores are filled to overflowing with goods of every kind—which visitors from other countries buy to bring home. We like to hear about how the American dollar is tendered abroad. What would we think of someone coming to tell us that we were an impoverished nation, sick in body and mind, and shamefully naked?

What then is Jesus trying to tell these people? What is he trying to tell us? He seems to be saying that wealthy people can indeed have another kind of poverty; that inhabitants of a city with a good eye clinic can have another kind of blindness; that people wearing nice sweaters and walking on beautiful carpets are nevertheless naked and baren in some other way.

What are such people to do? They are to buy gold from the risen Christ, every bit as good as the pearl of great price and treasure hidden in the field bringing one into the kingdom. Here it is refined gold, pointing to a life rid of impurities, whatever they may be. People are told to put on white garments, which does not mean getting a new white suit or a new white dress, but to have one's sins washed in the blood of Jesus so one may honorably appear in the presence of God and Jesus in the day of Christ's coming. They are told to medicate their eyes so they can really see what is going on around them—in their own lives, in the world, in the church (vv. 18–19). There is a seeing that is not seeing, just as there is a hearing that is not hearing. Jesus in his concluding words to the Laodiceans wants real hearing to take place (v. 22). Symbols here all aim at describing the new life in Christ. People who have this new life will not be lukewarm; they will not flag in zeal; they will be aglow in the Spirit; they will be continually serving the Lord.

Joshua, just before his death, called the people together for a renewal of the covenant. They had become lukewarm and needed the fire of Sinai rekindled. Joshua rekindled that fire at Shechem (Joshua 24). Israel made a covenant to serve the Lord, a covenant they and generations to follow had a hard time keeping, but when Joshua said, "Choose this day whom you will serve," the people responded with "We will serve the Lord, for he is our God." We have a new covenant in Jesus Christ that remains at the center of life between God and the church; it is a light unto our path and a security amidst every adversity. May we keep up our end of this covenant.

The world around us is heating up. There is a zeal of people with other religious beliefs, both here and abroad, people with civic and political beliefs that clash sharply with those undergirding our nation; with social beliefs and alternate lifestyles that undercut the family, and which hold no promise for the future, even as they held no promise in the past.

Jesus is the one "who is and who was and who is to come" (Rev 1:4, 8). "Jesus Christ is the same yesterday and today and forever" (Heb 13:8). Today is not a time to be neither hot nor cold about the claims of Christ, who was raised from the dead and speaks now from the heavenly throne. We need not be out of control with enthusiasm. But we do need a heavenly passion. On this day of worldwide communion, let us affirm our oneness with all who call upon the name of Jesus in sincerity and in truth, who are gathering around this table wherein one finds the presence of the living Christ. AMEN

14

"Olive Shoots around Your Table"[1]

Thanksgiving

Text: Psalm 128:3–4

Your wife will be like a fruitful vine
  within your house
Your children will be like olive shoots
  around your table
Thus shall the man be blessed
  who fears the Lord.

Psalm 128 is a "Song of Ascents" or "Pilgrim Song." There are fifteen of them in book 5 of the Psalter. They were sung as the pilgrim ascended Mount Zion to the temple where the great feasts were celebrated. This psalm appears to have been sung by the priest, who addresses his words to the men. Hear the entire psalm:

> Happy is everyone who fears the Lord
>   who walks in his ways
> You shall eat the fruit of the labor of your hands
>   you shall be happy, and it shall go well with you

---

1. Preached at the Covenant Congregational Church of Boston, Massachusetts, on November 23, 1975.

Your wife will be like a fruitful vine
    within your house
Your children will be like olive shoots
    around your table
Thus shall the man be blessed
    who fears the Lord
The Lord bless you from Zion
    may you see the prosperity of Jerusalem
    all the days of your life
May you see your children's children
    peace be upon Israel.

The psalm is one of blessing. The man who fears the Lord shall have food to eat and be happy. His wife will bear him many children who will sit around the table with the two of them like so many olive shoots. This man can hope to see the prosperity of Jerusalem all his days—a city free from attack and not in danger of going bankrupt (the psalm reflects the optimism of David and Solomon's time). In addition, this man in his older years may see grandchildren.

This is tenth-century Israel, when Israel for the first time was welded together into a single unit. It was a time of unprecedented prosperity, and the family—not the tribe—was the model for Israelites to emulate. To have your family together was to be greatly blessed by the Lord.

Such a picture comes easily into focus for most of us. Dad and Mom are celebrating one of the holiday feasts, and around the table sit children and grandchildren. It is no less a blessing today than it was then. If someone should happen upon such a scene they would say, "Isn't it wonderful that you can all be here together." It is our way of saying, "My, aren't you blessed by the Lord!"

There is something about having your children there at Thanksgiving or Christmas. You need the little ones, and when they are older you still want them there. Olive shoots grown bigger fit quite naturally around your table. I see no reason to find any fault with this. We are not dealing here with something superficial. Blood ties are thick, and the togetherness we feel as a family runs deep. I suspect it has been so in all ages. I have thanked God many times for the blessing coming from sitting around the family table—whether it was with my own mom and dad, grandma, and grandpa, or now with my wife and children. Perhaps you too have felt this way.

The family tells us who we are and where we come from. Stop and think about it. If someone asks you who you are, how do you answer? You might first give them your name, which may tie you to your family. If the person wants to know more, you might tell them who your parents are, or the name of your sister, if that will help. It happened to me recently that I became known because I was father to one of my children.

The "Where do you come from?" question is closely related. Our first answer might contain the name of a city, which in our country doesn't provide as much information as in Europe or other places, where mobility is less. You might then get to ethnic origin, and before long you will talk about being English, German, French, Swedish or of some other background. Today many are tracing their ethnic origins. If you are Swedish, you can go to the parish church or Emigrant Institute in Växjö and find out a great deal about your family tree. Even when talking about ethnic origins we are still talking about blood ties—about natural children and the degree of homogeneity we possess. Psalm 128 takes this for granted. It is husband and wife and their natural children.

If we read this psalm as a blessing upon such a family, fine. But what if you have a wife and she is unable to bear children? Or what if you, the husband, are unable to give her children? Today we realize it can be the man who creates an inability of his wife to get pregnant. Or suppose you have olive shoots around your table that are not your own? They may be foster children or adopted children or children belonging to someone else. And suppose you sit at table this year with an empty chair where Grandma, Grandpa, or one of your olive shoots used to sit, but is no longer with you. You may be all alone, with no husband, wife, or child. Is there no blessing for you? Do you not fear the Lord?

We have all sat at table at one time or another when we felt everyone was present. But we have also known times when the gathering was a fragmented one, when someone was particularly missed, or when someone joined the table from outside. We maybe resisted someone from outside the family joining our family at Christmas.

In the years following David and Solomon it was believed that Israel had pure origins. We hear this even from Isaiah and Jeremiah, who spoke of Israel as a "choice vine." Isaiah in his "Song of the Vineyard" tells how the Lord planted Israel as a choice vine; it was his "pleasant planting" (Isa 5:2, 7). But something happened. He looked for it to yield choice grapes, but it yielded wild grapes. Jeremiah, too, spoke this word from the Lord: "Yet I planted you as a choice vine, from the purest stock; how then did you turn degenerate and become a wild vine?" (Jer 2:21).

Oil Enough to Make the Journey

The idea that Israel was holy, a set-apart people, comes from Deuteronomy (Deut 7:6). But Deuteronomy is also the book of the Old Testament that speaks most clearly about sitting others around the family table. When Israelites go to the annual feasts at the central place of worship, they are not only to have their sons and daughters around the table, but are to invite male and female slaves, sojourners, orphans, widows, and pensioned Levites to join them (Deut 16:9–15). In the third-year charity tithe, which was to be celebrated in the towns, produce was to be set aside for the poor and needy. The surplus would be put in storage facilities to be doled out as needed. To this feast resident Levites, sojourners, orphans, and widows were to be invited, eating in gladness until they were filled (Deut 14:28–29; 26:12–13). This would bring blessing from the Lord.

The prophet Ezekiel, however, had another view of Israel's origins. He did not think Israel was "wholly of pure seed." He says Israel's father was an Amorite and his mother a Hittite. Israel, in fact, was an orphan cast out by alien parents into the field right after birth. There Yahweh saw her, lying in her blood, and took her up, telling her "Live! and grow up like a plant of the field" (Ezek 16:1–7). And so she did. No idyllic early family picture in the album for this prophet.

Jesus addressed the purity issue in a different way. In his day it was about the relationship between the Jews and Samaritans. You remember who the Samaritans were. They were an alien people brought in by the Assyrians to inhabit Samaria after the Northern Kingdom fell in 722, when surviving Israelites were carried off to faraway Assyria. These foreigners adopted the Jewish religion but were not Jewish. So a rivalry existed between the two groups that went on for centuries. Each had their own temple. Jews and Samaritans were not even first cousins!

To hear again the parable of the Good Samaritan (Luke 10:30–37) and to read about Jesus' visit with the Samaritan woman at Jacob's Well (John 4:1–42) is to realize that Jesus was hardly on the side of preserving Jewish homogeneity. The Samaritan traveler treated the wounded Jew in precisely the way the Lord treated Israel when finding her in the open field—the bandages, the oil, and the subsequent care are all verbal echoes of Ezekiel ringing in the ears. And what about that Samaritan woman from Sychar? After talking to Jesus she told her friends, and they invited Jesus to their table. We are told he stayed with them two days. Hospitality in both cases was to an alien. Yet these stories were remembered, told, and retold, in the

"Olive Shoots around Your Table"

hopes that Jews would turn the tables and reciprocate to alien neighbors in Samaria.

Later in the first century AD the Christian church, although established initially as a Jewish church, was rapidly becoming Gentile. A new chosen people was emerging and soon came boasting that they were superior. One hears this among the church fathers. But Paul has to remind the church at Rome that while some wild olive shoots were grafted on after holy branches of the tree were broken off, the root was still holy. He says, "Do not boast over the branches. If you do boast, remember that it is not you that support the root, but the root that supports you" (Rom 11:18).

Our Christian origins, if we are at all concerned about origins, are not pure. And as time went on, the Christian church became even more diverse—incorporating Greeks and Romans who previously worshiped Zeus, Artemis his daughter, and Apollo his son. About a thousand years later Christians in Scandinavia had fathers and mothers who worshiped Odin and Thor—Thor, you remember, was the one who in thunder and storms was throwing the hammer.

We are orphans and wild shoots all of us, and only by the grace of God were we spared abandonment and grafted into the community we are now in. We must not think of ourselves as a homogeneous race, as members of a homogeneous community, or as members of a homogeneous family. We are not pure seed. So let us welcome others from outside. In this holiday season we rejoice in the olive shoots around our table—our own, of course, but other wild shoots who are waiting, perhaps hoping, to be invited to sit at our table. Will we include them? AMEN

Being Faithful in the Christian Walk

15

What about Anger?[1]

Text: Matthew 5:21-22

You have heard that it was said to those of ancient times, "You shall not murder;" and "whoever murders shall be liable to judgment." But I say to you that if you are angry with a brother or sister, you will be liable to judgment; and if you insult a brother or sister, you will be liable to the council; and if you say, "You fool," you will be liable to the hell of fire.

Ever since the 1960s, I think, we have become particularly sensitive in America to expressions of anger, probably because anger then was vented on such a large scale. Across the land it burst forth, and our country was profoundly shaken by it. I often heard it said then that outbursts of anger were wrong—not to say immature, ungracious, and unloving. An angry young man was a wrong young man; an angry young woman a wrong young woman. Anger was much debated in the church. There it was said to be incompatible with the Christian gospel, and in the minds of some it was not to be tolerated.

If someone pointed out that God gets angry, or that Israel's prophets got angry—and they did not once, but often—the response was typically, "Well, that was the Old Testament; the teaching of the New Testament is different; there we are taught to love"—the idea being that anger and love are incompatible.

---

1. Preached at the Covenant Church in Menominee, Michigan, on August 29, 1993.

Psychologists at the same time were telling people to let their anger out. It was okay to be angry. They said people who got angry were healthier than those unable to express anger. Also, anger brought out into the open was more honest than anger kept inside, where it would fester and one day explode, maybe even bringing on mental illness. Psychologists were aware of the fact that open anger was not the only anger around. There was an anger resident in people who appear calm on the outside and say nary a harsh word, thought by some to be exemplary Christians.

Those who believed that Jesus was opposed to anger often quoted the verse chosen as our text for the morning: "If you are angry with a brother or sister you will be liable to judgment." What could be more clear? But others could quote Scripture saying something different. Paul says in Ephesians 4:26, "Be angry, but do not sin," a quote from Psalm 4:4.

We need to return for another look at our Gospel text. There we see that the meaning often given to the words is by no means clear. From ancient times this text has been difficult. Some early manuscripts of the New Testament have inserted the words "without cause," which gives the reading: "everyone who is angry with his brother (or sister) *without cause* will be liable to judgment." That changes things a bit. Now it is not getting angry that makes one liable to judgment, but getting angry without cause. This reading is found in the King James Bible. In the RSV and NRSV the reading appears in a footnote.

Why the expanded reading? Biblical scholars say it was to make the passage more clear, which is a simple answer to a complex problem. A better answer is that the verb "to be angry" in Greek, which is ὀργίζω, in this case probably means "make angry, provoke, irritate." Jesus is talking about one who "is provocative," not one who simply becomes angry.

This is the meaning of a similar verb in Ephesians 6:4, where Paul says, "And fathers, do not provoke (μὴ παροργίζετε) your children to anger, but bring them up in the discipline and instruction of the Lord." There is an anger of a father (or mother) toward children that is not right, and should be avoided. Paul also says in another of his letters, "Fathers, do not provoke (μὴ ἐρεθίζετε) your children, or they may lose heart" (Col 3:21). This is the anger being talked about in Jesus' Sermon on the Mount.

We all know about anger that is unwarranted, anger that is clearly wrong. We have words for people who show it, calling them contentious, troublesome, cantankerous, quarrelsome, belligerent, and the like. Whether it be toward a brother, a sister, children, or a friend—even a stranger on the street—one should not be angry so as to provoke or irritate, which is to be angry without cause. One should not use inflammatory language one knows will make another angry. Jesus goes on to give two words people used to be provocative, Ῥακά, and Μωρέ "You fool" may not do the second word justice, but I know some for whom being called "stupid" would. There are other English words more obscene.

Being angry, then, is not wrong in and of itself. The Old Testament and New Testament are in perfect harmony on this point. And you might be surprised to know that the church fathers, who wrote on the subject, agreed that the New Testament has a stronger teaching on anger, vengeance, and judgment than the Old Testament. Irenaeus said that in the New Testament God's vengeance is more real, more rigid, and more enduring: in the New Testament, after death people are sent to hell! He was right.

God is more demanding of Christians—particularly pious Christians—than he is of unwashed sinners (see the book of Hebrews in the New Testament). Life under the new covenant calls for greater faith than life under the old, which means a higher quality of living. Jesus says in the Sermon of the Mount that our righteousness must be greater than that of the Pharisees and the best of the Gentiles.

Yet in both the Old Testament and New Testament we receive clear warnings about anger. Anger, as everyone knows, is dangerous, and we must know how to handle it. There are three clear biblical guidelines.

First, we must be slow to anger. We learn this from God. One of God's great attributes is that he is slow to anger (Exod 34:6). He is not easily provoked; he does not fly off the handle at the first sight of wrongdoing; he does not judge people in haste. He is patient in his anger. It is a virtue to be slow to anger. The book of Proverbs contains many proverbs on the subject. Proverbs 14:29 says, "Whoever is slow to anger has great understanding, but one who has a hasty temper exalts folly." And in Proverbs 15:18: "Those who are hot-tempered stir up strife, but those who are slow to anger calm contention." Again in Proverbs 16:32: "One who is slow to anger is better than the mighty, and one whose temper is controlled than one who captures a city." And in Proverbs 19:11: "Those with good sense are slow to anger, and it is their glory to overlook an offense." Ecclesiastes 7:9 advises against being quick to express anger: "it lodges in the bosom of fools." In the New Testament see James 1:19.

The second thing the Bible teaches about anger is that it must be controlled. This follows closely on being slow to anger, as we see with the two coming together in Proverbs 16:32. Being slow to anger is controlling your anger. But what about when your anger actually breaks forth? Then, too, it must be controlled. The Old Testament compares anger to fire. In fact, one Hebrew word meaning "to be angry" also means "to burn." The analogy is apt. Fire must be controlled; if it is not, it can do untold damage. Linda and I observed a huge fire a couple years ago in Berkeley and Oakland. There have been others in California. Firefighters from distant places must be brought in to help put out such fires, and even then the task is difficult. The same is true with anger. If anger gets out of control, it can do enormous damage. There is great loss, some of which may never be recovered. Others may have to be brought in to bring things under control. And once again, it may prove a difficult undertaking.

There is controlled anger and an anger that is uncontrolled. Usually when we say a person "loses his temper" we mean that the person has allowed his or her anger to get out of control. Losing one's temper, then, is not simply becoming angry. It is "really losing it," as we say. The Old Testament warns against passionate or uncontrolled anger. Psalm 37:8 says, "Refrain from anger, and forsake wrath" (RSV and NRSV). The verb is an intensive, so a better reading would be "Refrain from passionate anger . . ." Proverbs 29:11 says: "A fool gives full vent to anger, but the wise quietly holds it back."

It is true that God sometimes shows consuming anger (Deut 32:22), but the Bible never gives us that right. No person is righteous enough to vent an all-consuming anger. No one has insight enough to consume another. God can do it, but we cannot. One way to control anger is by listening while we are angry. If we cannot hear what the other person is saying in our anger, we are usually out of control. This is especially important when parents get angry with their children. But it applies to anger with anyone. Be angry, but listen to what the other person is saying.

The third warning the Bible gives about anger is that it must not last. Anger is a legitimate human response, but it must get out and be done with. Here we see the danger in carrying long-term grudges. Legitimate anger is out and over with; illegitimate anger festers inside like a sore that won't heal. The Lord once again is our best example, having an anger that does not last. Psalm 30:5 says about the Lord: "For his anger is but for a moment; his favor is for a lifetime." Good advice for us all: Let your grace last forever, and your anger be momentary. In Psalm 103:9, again referring to the Lord, it says, "He will not always accuse, nor will he keep his anger forever."

Thankfully God in his anger—which is always a righteous anger—will not last forever.

The prophets told people that after the calamitous fall of the nation that the Lord would not keep his anger forever. In Jeremiah, the Lord is heard to say, "I will not be angry forever" (Jer 3:12). Micah said earlier this is because the Lord delights in steadfast love (Mic 7:18 RSV). Steadfast love, praise God, is forever.

In the Eph 4:26 passage, where Paul quotes a psalm about being angry but not sinning, he adds: "Do not let the sun go down on your anger." Anger must abate, and it is good policy not to carry it over into the next day. This is a verse my grandmother taught me, and it is excellent advice. I remember as a young boy going into my mother's bedroom at night and getting things settled before she and I went to sleep. As a result, the next morning began fresh and new.

I could not offer better advice to married couples. Get your anger out and over with. Settle it, if at all possible, by the end of the day. There is just one difficulty, and that is if you have an argument right before going to bed. That can be a problem because you need a cooling-off period, and the hour may be late. If the argument occurs at 11:00 p.m., the process needs to be hurried up. Nevertheless, it is true that if you wake up in the morning with yesterday's troubles remaining in yesterday, you are certain to have a better day and also more joy in life.

Love and anger are not incompatible. We need to be angry once and a while—there being wrongs in our families, in our communities, and in other people that need to be righted. We have heard, have we not, about righteous anger? Our text for the morning is teaching us is to refrain from provocative anger, which is anger without cause. Such anger resides in troubled souls in need of salvation. When we do get angry, let us simply remember to be slow to anger; to keep our anger under control; and never to let it last. AMEN

16

"To Obey Is Better Than Sacrifice"[1]

Text: 1 Samuel 15:22

Has the LORD *as great delight in burnt offerings and sacrifices*
  as in obeying the voice of the LORD*?*
Surely, to obey is better than sacrifice
  and to heed than the fat of rams."

Bringing sacrifices to the Lord seems a bit strange to most of us today—the idea of coming with grain or an animal to burn on an altar. Sometimes the whole animal was consumed on the altar; sometimes the priest got a choice portion; and sometimes most of the meat was consumed by the worshiper, his family, and invited guests. Among ancient people it was a way of life. Sacrifices were gifts to the gods—in Israel to the one God—who received them with gratitude, much in the way gifts we give are received by other people. We give gifts to please; it may be a way of saying thank you; it may pave the way for a future favor; or it may be all of the above.

Today we do not bring animals to burn on the altar—though occasionally people will indulge in "roast preacher" after the service is over, but usually at a safe distance from the holy place. That, incidentally, is their way of saying, "No thanks."

Yet none of us are strangers to gift-giving, which is what sacrifice is all about. There is the schoolgirl who brings an apple to the teacher; there is the young man who gives a Valentine box of candy to his sweetheart; there

---

1. Preached at the Salem Covenant Church in Worcester, Massachusetts, on February 14, 1982.

"To Obey Is Better Than Sacrifice"

is also the old man who gives Valentine candy to his sweetheart; businesspeople take their clients out for dinner; the pastor is invited to dinner, and someone may even buy him or her a new suit of clothes. When I pastored in farm country years ago, I was given an occasional package of bacon or a side of beef—which gets closer to the biblical practice.

Ancient religion devoted much energy to pleasing gods who were jealous, capricious, and unpredictable. People believed they could win their favor by elaborate gifts, yes, even coerce them into doing what they wanted.

The negative side of this, incidentally, is behaving like spoiled children who perform tantrums in order to bend parents into doing what they want them to do. This is the origin of fasting and self-mutilation, which were thought to evoke the god's pity. Self-mutilation was practiced in Baal religion, as we know from the Elijah incident on Mount Carmel (1 Kgs 18:28), but this was roundly rejected in Israel because it was a holy people (Deut 14:1–2). Nevertheless, sacrifices were routinely made to God, and we are told that he delighted in the smell of smoke (Gen 8:20–21).

The most remembered sacrifice in the Old Testament was when God told Abraham to offer up his only son Isaac, but as things turned out, a ram was substituted at the last minute for the lad (Gen 22). We learn from this incident something important about sacrifice. God can get along without human sacrifices; he substituted a ram for Isaac, but in a future day he would sacrifice his only Son for the sins of the world. The test here in Genesis was whether Abraham would be obedient to the Lord's command. It is all part of a single act. For Abraham to sacrifice is to obey; to obey is to be willing to sacrifice, tie up Isaac on the altar and raise his knife into the air. This great paradox of faith, as Søren Kierkegaard called it, captured the Danish thinker in his little classic, *Fear and Trembling*.

But then we come to Samuel, who teaches us what is more important. Samuel says to Saul: "To obey is better than sacrifice, and to heed than the fat of rams." Poor Saul. Abraham was put to the test and passed. Saul was tested and failed. Actually, Saul failed twice. Samuel's speech is the second of two lectures given to the Israelite king—both on the same subject. The first is recorded in 1 Samuel 13. On this earlier occasion Samuel had promised to meet Saul at an appointed time, when together they would sacrifice to the Lord before doing battle with the Philistines.

Though the biblical writer tells the story from Samuel's point of view, I must confess to having some sympathy for Saul. Samuel had promised to meet him in seven days, and when the seven days were up, Samuel was not there. Have you ever waited for someone who promised to meet you at a certain time, and did not show? It happened to me just recently. I waited in the cold for a friend at Harvard Square at a predetermined place at an hour that was convenient for him. He did not come. So finally I left.

It may be that time in antiquity was more like time currently in Africa, where things happen when they happen. I was in Zaire this past August speaking at an African pastors' conference, and waiting there is "the name of the game." Watches are worn mainly for status. Keeping time by hours and minutes is for us in the West; it is not for them. I asked someone about this when we were waiting for a friend, and was told he would come when he would come. But surely we could not wait indefinitely. No, but we must wait a while, although it was not clear how long.

At any rate, Saul's volunteer army was beginning to scatter; a sacrifice must be made before going to battle. And Samuel was not there. So Saul went ahead with the sacrifice. Just then Samuel appeared. Saul gets a lecture on not obeying the command of the Lord, which of course had come to him earlier via Samuel.

Now again in a battle with the Amalekites Saul is told not to take prisoners or keep any of the spoil. He does both. The spoil, he says, was to be a sacrifice to the Lord. As for sparing King Agag, he may have intended to have some "fun" with him, which was common in antiquity. Recall how the Philistines treated Samson after they captured him (Judg 16:25). This time the indictment against Saul was complete. Samuel says:

> Has the Lord as great delight in burnt offerings and sacrifices
>   as in obeying the voice of the Lord?
> Surely, to obey is better than sacrifice
>   and to heed than the fat of rams.

Samuel had learned the lesson on obedience early in life. There were memories of the Shiloh sanctuary where Eli was priest and where he was raised. Eli spent much time sacrificing to the Lord. So did his sons. Problem was his sons took more than their share of the meat (1 Sam 2:12–17), so much that they and their father became fat (2:29; 4:18). That was not all. Hophni and Phinehas were living loose with women at the sanctuary. So the Lord brought an end to it all. The Philistines defeated the Israelites in battle, the ark of the covenant was captured, and Eli's two reckless sons were killed. When the old priest heard the news, he fell over dead.

Eli was forewarned about a coming judgment from the young Samuel, when Samuel reported to him a word from the Lord received during the

"To Obey Is Better Than Sacrifice"

night. The Lord said, "Therefore I swear to the house of Eli that the iniquity of Eli's house shall not be expiated by sacrifice or offering forever" (1 Sam 3:14). So much for sacrifice. Samuel learned this lesson and learned it well. From this time on prophets were adamant on obedience being more important than sacrifice. It is not too much to say that the message of all the later prophets is encapsulated in this one word of Samuel to Saul.

Prophets in Israel continually say, "Hear the word of the Lord," and what they want is active hearing. The Hebrew word for "hear" also translates as "obey." You have heard mother or someone else say to you, "Why didn't you listen to what I said?" Well, you did listen, but you did not obey. We are too accustomed to passive listening. Some people like to have the radio on while they are studying. I don't, but some do. Then there is the background music in the supermarkets and the dentist's office. When you sit in the waiting room while your car is getting worked on, you have to be provided with television. If no one else is in the waiting room, I tell them to turn it off. Listening here requires no response whatever.

The kind of hearing the Old Testament prophets are talking about is active hearing, hearing that results in action, obedience, or both. I am talking about the kind of hearing you do when the telephone rings and you go to answer it. I am talking about the kind of hearing volunteer firemen do when the horn blows or a message comes over their CB radio. In ancient times the sound of the trumpet called people to action. Today in Africa it is the drum.

Jesus, too, is every bit as concerned about obedience. He says to people: "He who has ears to hear, let him hear." One of his parables is about two sons who are asked to go out and pull grapes. Both hear the father's words, but only one does the father's will and obeys. And at the end of the Sermon on the Mount Jesus tells the assembled that it is not enough to listen to his teachings; what matters is whether one does them. Again obedience is the bottom line.

The problem seems always to be with us. It lay at the heart of Dietrich Bonhoeffer's *Cost of Discipleship*, written during the early years of Nazi socialism in Germany. Bonhoeffer found to his sorrow that when the Nazis came to power the church, despite correct doctrine, did nothing. It did not act; it did not obey; it did not really follow Jesus. In the minds of most people it was thought that "only those who believe can obey." In other words, you have to first get your thinking straight; you first must seek to understand the Bible more; you must first have the right doctrine; you must first be sure of God's will; then you can obey.

Problem was it wasn't working. People who knew what was right failed to act. So he turned the thesis around in his book, saying, "only those who obey can believe." Real believers are people who obey. Discipleship comes when one leaves their nets, gets up from the tax table, climbs down from the sycamore tree, and follows Jesus.

Life in the church is little different when it comes to obeying God's commands and the teachings of Jesus. You had better not come and put your offering in the plate if you have alienated a friend or neighbor by provoking them with obscene language (Matt 5:22–26); you should not sit comfortably through communion if you have failed to examine yourself, as Scripture says you must (1 Cor 11:27–32); you can also stop singing great hymns of praise to God if you are eating lamb and beef, rubbing your skin with the finest oil, and drinking goblets of wine and are not grieved over ruin of your community, or your nation (Amos 6:4–6). Amos had harsh words for the people of Israel when they put worship ahead of justice and righteousness. Hear his words from the Lord:

> I hate, I despise your festivals
> > and I take no delight in your solemn assemblies
> Even though you offer me your burnt offerings and grain offerings
> > I will not accept them
> And the offerings of well-being of your fatted animals
> > I will not look upon
> Take away from me the noise of your songs
> > I will not listen to the melody of your harps
> But let justice roll down like waters
> > and righteousness like an everflowing stream.
> (Amos 5:21–24)

Obedience and giving gifts to God can and should go hand in hand. Nevertheless, it is well to remember that if it comes down to one or the other, in God's economy obedience is more important than sacrifice. AMEN

17

Love Is Something You Do[1]

Text: Romans 5:8

But God proves his love for us in that while we still were sinners Christ died for us.

I commonly resist sermons on the topic of love because I have always felt love is so deep that one runs the risk of trivializing it by talking about it. Perhaps the best way is to attack the subject indirectly. Profound experiences in life are spoiled when we try to talk about them. Love, by its very nature, is demonstrative, and although the Greeks wrote much about love, you and I—if we are honest—would rather someone show us love than talk to us about love.

I have noticed in the Bible—and I am sure it is also true outside the Bible—that passages where love is most obvious do not contain the word. Take Jesus' parable of the prodigal son. Where do we see any better the love of a father for his sons—both the younger and older one—and the love God has for his wayward children? The word *love* does not even appear in the parable. Take also the parable of the lost sheep (Luke 15:3–7). If we look at Jesus' encounters with people such as Zacchaeus (Luke 19:1–10), the Samaritan woman at the well (John 4:1–42), or the woman caught in adultery (John 8:1–11), do we not see love being shown? Gospel writers do not need to point out that Jesus loves people.

It is rare to hear Paul discussing love as he does so beautifully as in 1 Corinthians 13. In his epistles John also talks about love—the love of

---

1. Preached at the Covenant Church in Hopkinton, Massachusetts, on June 27, 1982.

God and love of one to another. But most love preserved on the pages of Scripture is a love unmentioned; it is love being shown.

Some years ago the Presbyterian preacher Dr. Frederick Speakman wrote a book titled *Love Is Something You Do*. In it he said that love in Scripture is something more than feeling or human desire; it is something you do, or something you are expected to do. God shows love in his saving deeds. Jesus acts out love in healing and ultimately in a sacrifice of grand proportion. Christians, similarly, are to express their love in living out the terms of the new covenant. Our text says that God "proves his love for us in that while we still were sinners Christ died for us." In the great act of giving up his Son for our salvation, he demonstrated a profound love for us. Love was something God did—for us and for the world.

You have heard, no doubt, about the three different words the Greeks used for "love": *eros, filia,* and *agapē*. *Eros* was said to be the love deep within the human soul surging outward in search of someone or something for oneself. The Greeks used this for love people had for the gods. *Filia* was more linear; it was love between friends, although it could also be the love gods show toward people. *Agapē* was "love reaching down" to lift up someone below you—used by the Greeks for the love gods showed toward human beings.

Other distinctions can also be made. *Eros* is passionate love, a desire, a feeling, or, as one scholar put it, "an intoxicating love that puts an end to reason and reflection, and sets all the senses in a frenzy." It is not necessarily a base love implied in the English word *erotic*—although it probably would include X-rated movies and what appears on pages of many of today's magazines and paperbacks. *Eros* is also that natural and beautiful attraction lovers feel for each other, or which anyone might feel toward another who possesses qualities one deeply appreciates.

The philosophers of ancient Greece, Plato and Aristotle, explained *eros* in nonsensual terms; for them it was a kind of "creative inspiration," where one is transported beyond reason into a mystical and supersensual world. *Agapē* was the least important word for the Greeks. Quite often it meant no more than "to be satisfied with something." It had no real importance in religion; Greek religion—like other ancient religions—had more to do with *eros*.

When the Old Testament was translated into Greek, beginning in the third century BC, the translators most often chose *agapē* for *ahab*, which was the Hebrew word for "love." Hebrew had only this one word, and as one might expect in a language with a small vocabulary, the term carried more freight. *Ahab* could mean passionate love of a man and woman; selfless loyalty or friendship; or resolute adherence to righteousness. It expresses God's love for Israel, and the love God expected in return—to him and to others, even to the stranger (Deut 10:12—11:1).

The most distinguishing characteristic of love in the Old Testament is that it is an act; it is not so much how you feel; it is something you are supposed to do. This meaning is expressed by Jesus and writers of the New Testament. *Agapē* for Christians became demonstrated love, love that bent down to pick another up, love that showed faithfulness to the new covenant. Love was charity, benevolence, hospitality. Love was a duty.

So if we are going to understand what Christian love is all about, we cannot simply talk about feeling and desire, even though both components are present. We must talk about something within us that transcends feeling and desire. Love is a duty we have toward God and toward one another. Love is something we do.

How do we know that love is a duty? We know it because in the Bible love is commanded. The Old Testament says: "You shall love the Lord your God with all your heart, and with all your soul, and with all your might" (Deut 6:5). It says, "You shall love your neighbor as yourself" (Lev 19:18). In the New Testament Jesus says, "I give you a new commandment, that you love one another. Just as I have loved you, you also should love one another" (John 13:34).

If love were only a feeling or desire, it would not have to be commanded. You either have it or you don't. Does anyone who loves their husband or wife, their girlfriend or boyfriend, have to be told to love them? Did anyone say in the very beginning that you were to love them? Does anyone have to tell you to love family and friends? You may need to be told to love your neighbor, but family and friends are loved naturally and spontaneously.

The very fact that the Bible commands love should be enough to tell us that this is not something we necessarily feel or desire. Feelings and desire could point us in a different direction entirely. Love is the Bible is something we must do.

There is an interesting law given to people in the Old Testament. It says:

> When you come upon your enemy's ox or donkey going astray, you shall bring it back. When you see the donkey of one who hates

you lying under its burden and you would hold back from setting it free, you must help to set it free. (Exod 23:4–5)

We are talking here about someone who hates you. Even if you do not hate them in return, chances are you don't like them. Nevertheless, you are to show charity by caring for the animal belonging to them. This is not a love you feel; it is love you do.

A similar law occurs in Deuteronomy, where the Israelite is not to ignore a stray animal belonging to a family member, friend, or neighbor, but return it to them. If the owner lives some distance away, or you do not know who the owner is, you are to care for it until the owner comes looking for it (Deut 22:1–4). So if you are to render assistance to your enemy, you should do no less for one who is your brother, neighbor, or friend. The point once again is that love can be commanded. It may not issue forth naturally; you may feel like acting in another way entirely.

A lawyer put Jesus to the test by asking how he might achieve eternal life. Jesus asks him, "What is written in the law?" The lawyer quotes two passages from the law that we just mentioned: "You shall love the Lord your God with all your heart, and with all your soul, and with all your strength, and with all your mind; and your neighbor as yourself." Jesus says, "Do this, and you will live" (Luke 10:25–28). He does not say, "Believe this," or "Feel this way," but "*Do* this!" What follows is the parable of the good Samaritan. Elsewhere in the New Testament love consists of feeding the hungry, giving the thirsty a drink, welcoming the stranger, clothing the unclothed, visiting the sick and those in prison (Matt 25:31–46). This is the demonstrative love taught to Israel.

Today the common gospel is "If it feels good do it," or "What feels good has to be right." But this not the gospel taught in the Bible. A lot of things feel good that we have no business doing. And things that feel good may not always be right. For Jeremiah, as for other prophets, loving God was doing what he least wanted to do—preaching what people did not want to hear; exposing himself to danger, persecution and death; suffering shame; and more. Jesus gives us a similar example, and Christian witnesses down through the ages have done the same.

Jesus said, "No one has greater love than this, to lay down one's life for one's friends" (John 15:13). This Jesus himself did. Did he feel like doing it? Did he desire such love? To imagine so is to miss the drama in his great sacrifice. Can we follow this Jesus in loving one another?

Love Is Something You Do

Will Rogers said he "never met a man [he] didn't like." Few of us can say this. We have certainly met persons we didn't love. But if we live under a love that can be commanded, and this love is something we must do, then we might begin to understand something about God's love, also the love of Jesus, who, while we were yet sinners, died for us. AMEN

18

The Indelicacy of Too-Ready Speech[1]

Text: Job 42:3

*"Who is this that hides counsel without knowledge?"
Therefore I have uttered what I did not understand,
things too wonderful for me, which I did not know.*

Thomas Kelly, a Quaker who lived in the early years of this century, wrote a thoughtful devotional book about "holy obedience" in which he said that Christians—and others as well—are often known to speak too quickly. He called this "the indelicacy of too-ready speech." We usually ay, "He or she spoke too soon," meaning that the person did not think before speaking, or that he or she spoke without knowing what they were saying. Words can get ahead of us, and when they do, others will not listen or else call us short, and we wish we had not spoken at all.

The Old Testament book of Job teaches us about the "indelicacy of too-ready speech." Job, has been through intense suffering; he knows he is innocent; he has not cursed God, but he is unable to find a mediator. The advice he gets from friends, which is that only sinful people suffer, is not right, so he cries out, "Let the Almighty answer me!" (Job 31:35).

Well, the Almighty does answer, out of a mighty whirlwind, but not to give Job an explanation for his suffering. Instead he unleashes a barrage of questions Job cannot answer (38:1—41:34). Was Job present at creation? Does he now know where to find everything? Has he entered the deep,

---

1. Preached at the Covenant Church of Thomaston, Connecticut, on February 5, 1984.

The Indelicacy of Too-Ready Speech

seen the gates of death, or traversed the place where light dwells and where storehouses of snow exist? Would Job know how to operate the created order? Does he know the ways of animals and birds, and could he provide for them? Can he take on the great land and sea monsters, Behemoth and Leviathan? At the end Job is sobered, and can only say, "I have uttered what I did not understand, things too wonderful for me, which I did not know . . . therefore I despise myself, and repent in dust and ashes" (42:3, 6). Job has asked too much; he has exceeded his understanding; he now knows the indelicacy of too-ready speech.

Earlier in the book his wife made this mistake. Job had been afflicted with sores from the sole of his foot to the crown of his head, and his wife said, "Curse God, and die" (2:9). Job reproached her for being a foolish woman. And what are we to say about Job's three friends, Eliphaz, Bildad, and Zophar, who also show misunderstanding and are later reproached for not speaking what is right about God (42:7–8)? At first, of course, they acted rather well. When they saw Job and did not recognize him in his terrible condition, they could only weep. Then they sat on the ground with him seven days and seven nights, during which time not a word was spoken, for "they saw that his suffering was very great" (2:13). Here were friends who did understand the indelicacy of too-ready speech.

One might also have a look at the prophet Ezekiel, moved by God's Spirit to preach to the exiles in Babylon. We are told that he went down to their makeshift quarters by the River Chebar, and "sat there among them, stunned, for seven days" (Ezek 3:15). Doubtless he sat in silence, as Job's friends did. Ezekiel had the added burden of having been told to speak God's word to a stubborn people. Here it was even more important to be silent before one speaks.

People in antiquity understood the danger of words running ahead of thinking and action: An old Akkadian proverb says: "What you say in haste you may regret later; exert yourself to restrain your speech."[2] In the Bible we get this advice: "Do you see someone who is hasty in speech? There is more hope for a fool than for anyone like that" (Prov 29:20). Jewish rabbis later said, "Listen twice, speak once."

I heard something similar just a couple days ago from a China missionary now living in retirement in Chicago. She told how missionaries cast out demons in control of people. Before they would call the demon

---

2. James B. Pritchard, ed., *Ancient Near Eastern Texts* (3rd ed; Princeton: Princeton University Press, 1969), 595.

out, they would gather together for prayer, asking God to cleanse them of any evil within themselves that might get in the way of God's saving work. They did this, and then called the demon out of the one who was possessed. It came out, and everyone in the village knew it, for the person was dramatically changed—from anger, erratic behavior, and even murder to good behavior. Opportunities for witness then became legion because everyone wanted to know what had happened, and they were told.

We recall how Jesus acted at the time Lazarus died. When Mary came running to tell him the news and say that had he been there her brother would not have died, Jesus, we are told, "was greatly disturbed in spirit and deeply moved" (John 11:33). He did not explain his delay, but simply asked where Lazarus had been laid. They took him there, and "Jesus wept" (v. 35).

People around him were talking, some speaking of Jesus' love for Lazarus, others saying, "Could not he who opened the eyes of the blind man have kept this man from dying?" (v. 37). Jesus, still deeply moved, says, "Take away the stone."

He and Martha then had a brief exchange—Martha speaking about the odor in the tomb and Jesus about seeing the glory of God. Jesus then offered a brief prayer, thanking God for already answering it. Then he called Lazarus forth, and the dead man came forth. Jesus is a man of few words—but what power in those words!

Jesus showed good sense also before Caiaphas, the high priest. People were making reckless statements right and left about him, and the high priest asked him to defend himself. He said nothing. Let their foolishness ring in their own ears! Then the high priest asked Jesus if he was the Christ. To be silent now would show contempt, and Jesus—like Paul some years later—was unwilling to show contempt of the high priest (cf. Acts 23:5). He simply said, "I am," and followed with a word about the Son of Man coming in power (Mark 14:53–62).

Mark follows by reporting Peter's words to the maid of the high priest, and then to some bystanders. We know Peter will speak without thinking. And he does. Three times he denies that he knows Jesus, the third time calling down a curse upon himself as if to authenticate his word. It is really a lie. The crowing of the cock tells him it is a lie. Peter has been guilty of too-ready speech. He is deeply sorry, and the tears he weeps says it all.

In our dealings with people today, particularly those who are suffering, would that we might keep from giving stock answers—whether ours or

The Indelicacy of Too-Ready Speech

those others are giving—too readily. It would be better to be quiet. Or to weep, as Job's friends did at first.

People ask why their loved one has died, why God has not answered their prayers, or why they must endure sickness, hardship, or trouble. At such times we must beware of always having to give reasons, or of giving an answer we have come up with to one of our own problems. We must beware of the indelicacy of too-ready speech.

When it comes to witnessing to the faith, if we are going to be a real help to people; if we are to bring people a truly saving word; if we intend to communicate a love that is genuine; and if we seek to correct them for wrongdoing, let us listen twice and speak once. Beware of the indelicacy of too-ready speech. People remain outside the church because we who are inside are insensitive, too right, and too all-knowing. If God can hold back answers, so can we. In a spirit of humility, then, let us proceed to a celebration of Holy Communion. AMEN

19

"Peace, Peace, When There Is No Peace"[1]

Text: Jeremiah 6:13–15

For from the least to the greatest of them
  everyone is greedy for unjust gain
And from prophet to priest
  everyone deals falsely
They have healed the wound of my people lightly
  saying, "Peace, peace," when there is no peace
Were they ashamed when they committed abomination?
  No, they were not at all ashamed
  they did not know how to blush
Therefore they shall fall among those who fall
  at the time that I punish them, they shall be overthrown
  says the LORD *(RSV).*

The life of the student can be stimulating. We have our eyes opened continually to new things and, if we are not lazy, we come to a deeper understanding of our world and ourselves. As seminary students we learn to talk about God and come to better understanding his Word as the Scripture reveals it to us. I have found this to be especially true with the book of Jeremiah. Every time I read it, something new appears that I had not seen before. Jeremiah's skill as a poet, his searching confessions, his utter frankness with

1. Preached in the chapel of the Near East School of Theology, Beirut, Lebanon, on March 16, 1965.

"Peace, Peace, When There Is No Peace"

God—being driven at one point to curse the day of his birth—command my admiration.

Sometimes I wish I could just sit back and admire him. He was a true man of God. His preaching was certainly a comfort to the exiles after Jerusalem had fallen, and his message has continued to have meaning for Christians over the generations, but what makes him so outstanding? Why is he the man that he was? Can we conclude about him, as some have said of Martin Luther, that he was psychotic?

I would suggest to you this morning something I have already suggested to myself, that Jeremiah was not unlike you or I who have been called to preach God's Word in today's world. He was a loyal citizen of Judah; he was afraid of what might happen if he spoke the truth; he argued with God about his call, not once but more than once; his protest as a young boy that he was unable to speak reminds us of Moses.

A book of the law found in the temple triggered off a reform under King Josiah. Why didn't Jeremiah join in with the others, among whom were priests and prophets, and celebrate the occasion? He didn't; he sat alone (Jer 15:16–17). Later he took elders and senior priests down into the Valley of Ben Hinnom and predicted a destruction of Jerusalem so complete that the valley would serve as a burial place because no other would be available. I feel a kinship to the man, knowing as he did that finding God's Word and studying it joyfully is far easier than preaching it. Yet Jeremiah went ahead and preached the Word. At times it was a struggle, but he preached it!

I have chosen as my text for the morning Jeremiah's words: "They have healed the wound of my people lightly, saying 'Peace, peace,' when there is no peace" (Jer 6:14). I have looked in vain for comforting words as I look ahead to my ministry in America, but all I see are these words about the false prophets of Jeremiah's day: "They have healed the wound of my people lightly, saying, "Peace, peace, when there is no peace." What an unpopular message to bring to people!

Jehu, after being anointed king by a disciple of Elisha, went out to battle against Joram of Israel and Ahaziah of Judah. Upon encountering Jehu, Joram asked, "Is it peace Jehu?" to which Jehu answered, "What peace can there be, so long as the many whoredoms and sorceries of your mother Jezebel continue?" (2 Kgs 9:22).

Jesus gave this answer to some who were looking for peace at his coming. He said, "Do not think that I have come to bring peace to the earth; I have not come to bring peace, but a sword" (Matt 10:34).

I should like to share with you some observations I have made about peace. First, peace cannot be made in isolation. It comes in unity, which the church is seeking so fervently today, and it can be a lasting peace only if it is firmly rooted in Jesus Christ, who turned out to be the Prince of Peace. There is a paradox in Jesus both not bringing peace and bringing true peace. For us, too, it will often mean taking a stand for what is right and opposing what is wrong, which is the only way of achieving true peace.

Secondly, peace cannot be "surface peace." Being a peacemaker is something very different from "keeping the peace." The latter is like taking aspirin to dull the pain, or avoiding the problem altogether. Jeremiah was not concerned with this kind of peace. If the nation's wound was to be healed, it must be dealt with at its source. Judah had a deeper sickness within.

Thirdly, as individuals called to preach God's Word, we must be prepared to carry a cross. Many of you already know, more than I, what it means to suffer with Christ. The minister in the past has been a man of stature in the community, some having traded the cross for a comfortable life keeping people happy and worship ongoing.

But this is changing. Identifying with those fighting for civil rights in Alabama does not bring one prestige among family and friends; for some it brings death. Let us pray then not only for a world united in peace, but a church so loyal to its Lord that it can show the world the road leading to lasting peace. AMEN

20

Sowing in Tears, Reaping with Shouts of Joy[1]

Lent

Text: Psalm 126:5–6

May those who sow in tears
  reap with shouts of joy
Those who go out weeping
  bearing the seed for sowing
Shall come home with shouts of joy
  carrying their sheaves.

In our psalm for this Sunday we have an age-old saying that has been preserved among people who work the land. Verse 5 is essentially a proverb, even though here in the psalm it is phrased as a blessing from the priest to the worshiper. The proverb would go:

> The one who sows in tears
>   shall reap with shouts of joy.

Like many proverbs, this one has a "flip side," which has been preserved among farmers over the centuries in Germany. They say:

---

1. Preached at the Covenant Church in Thomaston, Connecticut, on March 2, 1986.

> Do not laugh when you sow
> otherwise you must weep when you reap.

Proverbs do not apply to every situation in every age, but they are general truths that ring true again and again. Therefore if we are to be wise, we attempt to understand them and let them instruct us.

In the ancient world it was common to consider sowing seed as a time of mourning. There were even rites of mourning in fertility religions of the ancient Near East. We have examples from Egypt, Phoenicia, and Canaan, which the people of Israel came to possess. Seed must die when it is put into the ground, and the mourning is over the loss of much good seed. We see this idea preserved also in the New Testament. For example, Jesus says, "Very truly, I tell you, unless a grain of wheat falls into the earth and dies, it remains just a single grain; but if it dies, it bears much fruit" (John 12:24). He is talking about losing your life in order to find it. Paul, too, in speaking about the resurrection of the body, says, "Fool! What you sow does not come to life unless it dies" (1 Cor 15:36).

The Israelite people, when they took over the land, gave up ideas other fertility religions had about the gods dying at the time of planting, but they retained the idea that the seed dies when put into the ground, and that was something to be sad about.

This makes sense to farmers today, as I discovered when I was pastor in farm country out in California. Those of us who are town and city folk must appreciate how precious seed is to the farmer, particularly one not wealthy. He sacrifices to plant seed. Seed, after all, is like money in hand. It has value as food; the farmer to buy it has to pay money. And when the seed is put into the ground it is gone. What is more, one never knows whether it will bring a yield.

The farmer who puts his seed into the ground is making an investment; he is taking some risk. And if the seed be his total resource at the time, he may well shed a few tears when all has been planted. Again, for the proverb to make sense the farmer must be putting out all that he has. He will not most likely be a wealthy person able to plant seed and feel no pain if nothing comes at harvest time, though it is true that even wealthy people can mourn the loss of seed.

However, in the reversed form of the proverb it makes sense if the person planting is either wealthy, careless, or both. We see, for example, in the parable of the lost (prodigal) son an initial joy in spending "seed money," but later weeping when it comes to nothing.

Sowing in Tears, Reaping with Shouts of Joy

The Bible in many places expands the literal meaning of this proverb to make the truth apply more generally to all of life, to actions thought of as "sowing." The prophet Hosea speaks about the reckless people in Samaria who have done a poor job of choosing kings and princes, made their silver and gold into idols, and have broken the law and spurned the good. He says, "For they sow the wind, and they shall reap the whirlwind" (Hos 8:7).

If sowing in life is done with too much merriment—assuming the merriment is a reckless sort where one does not weigh the significance of what one is doing—then a day will come when there will be much weeping. We talk, do we not, of "sowing wild oats"?

On the other hand, we have all known instances where one gives up the very last of what one has, and does so with a heavy heart—perhaps also with weeping—and yet, with a proper frame of mind, with faith, hope, and trust that good will come, some good does come; in fact, there is a harvest and with it great shouts of joy.

I think of that story in 1 Kings 17 where Elijah goes to the widow of Zarepath, which is near Sidon, because the drought is bad and now there is famine. Elijah has been sent there by the Lord to get food from the woman. He arrives, and upon meeting the woman he asks for some water and bread. She is out gathering sticks, something you see today in that country, and she tells Elijah that she has nothing baked, only a handful of meal in a jar and a little oil in a cruse. She says she is going to prepare that for herself and her son, and then die.

Elijah, however, is a bold sort of fellow, and asks her first to make him a cake, then afterwards make for herself and her son. He tells her that she will not run out of food and oil. The women did so, and it happened just as Elijah had said. She did not run out. The real joy, however, did not come until later, but before that came more weeping. The little boy took sick and died. But Elijah restored him to life. There was sowing with tears, but reaping with shouts of joy.

Jesus tells his followers that the life of discipleship will not be easy. In fact, it will be difficult at precisely those times when others are having an easy time of it. But he says, "Blessed are you who weep now, for you shall laugh . . . Woe to you who are laughing now, for you will mourn and weep" (Luke 6:21b, 25b).

I do not think it necessary to look for ways in which we can weep as we sow in life. It is enough, surely, to accept weeping when it comes. It is also enough to understand that a life lived with integrity, with principle, with sacrifice and selfless love toward others may bring us nothing of this world's treasure. It may bring only tears. But if our sowing is the right kind of sowing, there will be a harvest out ahead and with that harvest a time of shouting for joy.

We could talk about spending "seed money" on things we feel are of long-term value, but which make us cry when it depletes our savings. I think of spending money on our children's education; I think of giving up seed money for the church, for missions, for a friend or neighbor in need, when we might keep that money for ourselves. We are currently faced with the decision of what to do with some money given to the church. If we sow it properly, some may be weeping, for it will be gone! But there will be shouts of joy if a harvest comes in. We need to think about this.

It pains me to have to tell you this, but I have just returned from Chicago where there is sorrow and some weeping because of what we are reaping at our denominational college. A few years ago there was much merriment at the school, but amidst report after report of good news, we now come to find out that our school spent $43,847 over budget for advertising; hired a new vice president, gave him a fancy title so he could raise funds, even though at the time there was no money in the budget for the hiring—the cost here being $37,581; no internal controls were in place to monitor the changeover of part-time student employment to full-time employment, the cost here was $201,559 over budget; and insufficient checks on telephone calls, use of credit cards, etc. put the school over budget to the tune of $52,987. The list goes on. We now know that our school has incurred a debt of $2 million. Unofficial reports put it at three times that amount.

Well, the party is over. The president has resigned; the board is partially to blame, and our school is in real trouble. It has sown the wind, and reaped the whirlwind. There is sorrow and weeping. We are being asked to be supportive, to give more money, and take a positive view about it all. The truth is we really don't know what is going to happen in the future.

This past week a prodigal ruler in the Philippines has come to an unhappy end, reaping what he has sown: corruption, poverty for millions of his people, and even murder. People now want to recover the stolen billions he has taken away, and why not? He was caught stealing the election.

What are you sowing in your life? In your family life? In the life of the church? In affairs of the world? Are you sowing seeds of kindness? Are you sowing in word and deed the good news about Jesus? The truth in this case may make people weep when they realize what hopeless lives they are living. It may make you weep too. You young people, be careful what you sow. If you are reckless now, there will be bitterness and sorrow later on. Take your tears now, make the sacrifices asked of you, give up foolish pleasures for quality living, and shouts of joy will be yours when you reap the harvest. And let us all, in this Lenten season, be sobered by the sacrificial life and death of Jesus, who wept for a later joy, and wept that we might have life, and have it more abundantly. AMEN.

21

Mayonnaise, Mediators, and the Ministry of Barnabas[1]

Text: Acts 9:26–27

When he [Paul] had come to Jerusalem, he attempted to join the disciples; and they were all afraid of him, for they did not believe that he was a disciple. But Barnabas took him, and brought him to the apostles, and described for them how on the road he had seen the Lord, who had spoken to him, and how in Damascus he had spoken boldly in the name of Jesus.

IN A BOOK PUBLISHED a few years ago titled, *Mayonnaise and the Origin of Life*,[2] Harold J. Morowitz, professor of molecular biophysics and biochemistry at Yale University, discusses the physical properties and structures of certain things we eat, such as salad dressing, giving new insights also into the makeup of the living cell.

In one essay, which has the same title as the book, Morowitz makes an observation known to all who use French cookbooks, namely, that mayonnaise has only three constituent parts: vegetable oil, egg yolk, and vinegar. Had I been told this before I would have been unimpressed, but my interest quickened when I found out that this smooth and harmonious food would

---

1. Preached at the Covenant Church in Thomaston, Connecticut, on January 19, 1986.

2. Harold J. Morowitz, *Mayonnaise and the Origin of Life: Thoughts of Minds and Molecules* (New York: Scribner, 1985).

Mayonnaise, Mediators, and the Ministry of Barnabas

not be possible were it not for the egg yolk and the unique properties it possesses.

The egg yolk contains amphiphiles, which are molecules having diverse structures enabling them to attract substances that otherwise will not mix. In the case of mayonnaise, oil and vinegar—vinegar being basically water—are substances that will not mix. Thus the old saying: "water and oil don't mix." The term *amphiphiles* is Greek, its literal meaning being "something that loves both kinds." In the case of the egg yolk the molecular structure is such that one end is attracted to oil and the other end to vinegar/water. It therefore has the ability to bring oil and vinegar together, defying the saying that "water and oil do not mix." In mayonnaise they do.

Today we know more precisely the physical properties and structures of substances, yet as long ago as 1807 it was known that the egg yolk could be used to blend oil and water. I suppose what impresses me most about this new scientific information is that amphiphiles are contained in the most basic cell structures; they are requisites for life and are as important as proteins or DNA.

Scientists today are much taken up with the study of amphiphiles. They are proposing new theories in biogenesis, and it is now clear that molecules of this special type are at the very base of electromagnetic theory. Morowitz says that even though the term has yet to make the standard dictionaries (1985), we will be hearing a lot about amphiphiles in the days and years to come.

I expect it will only be a matter of time until social scientists lay hold of this observation, for there can be little doubt that individuals have the same sort of bonding ability in social groups that the egg yolk has in mayonnaise. What I mean is that certain individuals—maybe all individuals—have within them a structure of personality enabling them to bond people, who, for whatever reason cannot bond together on their own.

Individuals have dominant qualities, which, instead of attracting them to others, repel them. Also, we know that fear, earlier experiences in life, and hidden anxieties, make it impossible or nearly so for certain people to mix with certain other people. What we need in such a case is some "middle person" to bring them together.

Such a middle person—or mediator—in the early church was Barnabas. He had that certain something that "loves both kinds." Were it not for Barnabas, or another the likes of him, Paul may never have been integrated into the Antioch church, and may never have set out on the missionary journeys he embarked upon.

We read the story of Paul's pilgrimage in the book of Acts where we see that after his conversion and a brief stay in Damascus, where he first preached Christ to the Jews, and perhaps also after a visit to Arabia (Gal 1:17), he sought to join the disciples at Jerusalem. But they were afraid of him, wanting no part of this man who dragged Christians off to prison and had overseen their violent deaths.

Enter Barnabas. He takes Paul by the hand to meet Christians in the Jerusalem church. Because of this important middleman the church accepts Paul and he is able to preach in their midst (Acts 9:26–28). Paul did not stay long in Jerusalem, but just being there was important for him and the church. We know that later Paul had to return to Jerusalem and be himself the middleman in working out problems concerning a ministry to the Gentiles (Acts 15). What is more, Luke says the church had peace and was built up after Paul had been at Jerusalem (Acts 9:31).

Barnabas proved later to be an important mediator when he became pastor at Antioch. He saw that the task was too big for him, so he summoned Paul, who had gone back to Tarsus, and the two became co-pastors. Soon after, the Antioch church sent Paul and Barnabas out on a missionary journey—the first of three for Paul that became so important in the life of the early church.

Professor John Weborg of the North Park Theological Seminary preached an ordination sermon at the Covenant Annual Meeting in 1978 on the mediating role of Barnabas, which was later published.[3] In it he said,

> Barnabas had a very simple apostolic vocation. He was a place-finder for the unplaced and the displaced . . . [He] had that awkward and painful task of being the middleman, a mediator, a redeemer, suffering the wounds of those against whom he had to speak because their suspicions were keeping from them one in whom God had done a mighty work.

John is referring to the role Barnabas played in bringing Paul into the church—particularly at Jerusalem—and says this required temerity and courage. But those were the gifts this man possessed. He had that something which "loves both kinds."

In the Old Testament it is the prophets who are assigned the task of bringing God and people together. One gains the impression from reading

---

3. *The Covenant Companion* (June 1, 1979), 3–5.

the prophets that God and the Israelites are so unlike each other that they cannot possibly get together; they are like oil and vinegar. What they needed was a "man of God," a "messenger of God," which is what the prophet was.

If we go back farther, we discover that there was no more prominent mediator in Israel than Moses. We see his role as mediator in the Old Testament books of Exodus and Deuteronomy, where not once but more than once God becomes so angry with his people that he wants to consume them in one fiery moment. On one occasion, after the people made a golden calf, God offers to begin again with Moses (Deut 9:14). Perhaps through Moses he might finally succeed in building himself a nation. Moses wisely rejects the idea. True mediator that he was, Moses takes the side of the people and asks God to withhold his anger, although he does appeal, it is true, to God's public image among the Egyptians. What will they say when they hear that all the Israelites have been destroyed? Will there not be much gloating in the streets of Memphis? God relents.

Samuel, Amos, Hosea, and Jeremiah are the other great mediators between God and his people. And then comes Jesus, whose task it was to bring together, in that great act of atonement, God and a world hostile to him.

Deep alienation exists today between God and humankind. Alienations exist also between nations, cultures, ethnic groups, and individuals in general. Perhaps these are built into the molecular structure of things; in any case, alienation and hostility are there, and they cannot be bridged except for individuals like the good Barnabas who step in and bring people together.

In America we make much of the fact that our strength as a nation derives from our differences, and I think we realize, too, that differences in the church give us not only beauty and vitality, but provide us with strength. Still there has to be people who "love both kinds." Perhaps it is possible that each of us, in certain situations at least, can "love both kinds." If so, we need be alerted to those situations where people are alienated from God; where two friends of ours cannot get along with each other; where there is a rift between someone we know and love, and the church we know and love; where natural attachments are felt to people tied to this world, someone will not be brought to Jesus Christ unless a middleman or middlewoman does the job.

We are talking here about basic evangelism, about winning people to faith in Jesus, about building up the body of Christ that is so much in need of reconciling work among its members. Because of high goals set up for those of us who confess Jesus Christ, we may tire and become frustrated at being asked to do something we think we cannot do. But from Barnabas we see the importance of doing whatever we are capable of doing, things that may turn out to be not so difficult if only we attempt to do them. A new person coming into the church is ever so grateful for just one person, who, with ease and unpretentiousness serves as a bridge between themself and a group still very strange. Children are natural mediators to other children, also to certain adults, and often to children and adults outside our fellowship. May our church then be like mayonnaise. With more "egg yolks" it will certainly have peace and be built up like the New Testament church. AMEN

22

"When the Son of Man Comes, Will He Find Faith?"[1]

Text: Luke 18:1–8

Then Jesus told them a parable about their need to pray always and not to lose heart. He said, "In a certain city there was a judge who neither feared God nor had respect for people. In that city there was a widow who kept coming to him and saying, 'Grant me justice against my opponent.' For a while he refused; but later he said to himself, 'Though I have no fear of God and no respect for anyone, yet because this widow keeps bothering me, I will grant her justice, so that she may not wear me out by continually coming.'" And the Lord said, "Listen to what the unjust judge says. And will not God grant justice to his chosen ones who cry to him day and night? Will he delay long in helping them? I tell you, he will quickly grant justice to them. And yet, when the Son of Man comes, will he find faith on earth?"

Throughout the Bible are two themes implicitly if not explicitly together. They build on the relationship between God and his people, the covenant, which is unique to Judaism and Christianity. No other religion knows of such a covenant. For Christians it is the new covenant promised by Jeremiah (Jer 31:31–34) and claimed later by the church. These two themes are (a) the vindicating and saving activity of God over all adversaries and

---

1. Preached at the Mar Thoma Church, Chennai, India, on July 10, 2005.

the power of evil, and (b) the faith resident among people who profess to worship this God.

Over the years the church has debated, e.g., in baptism, which is more important. Is it God's divine work, or is it our faith—the faith of the one being baptized or the faith of parents bringing their infant to baptism? These debates usually go nowhere simply because it becomes clear in the end that both divine grace and faith mysteriously hang together. What is more, the saving power of God can only be known in faith: faith anticipates its coming; faith welcomes its appearance; and faith remembers how this power has transformed life in times past.

So long as God acts and people show faith, there is no problem. Yet repeatedly there is a breakdown in confidence, if you will, which the Bible bears witness to time and time again. It is a problem not unknown in our own day. From the human side there is the worry that God will not hear our cries or deliver us from our distress, leading to a loss of courage on our part, and worse yet, a loss of hope. God, on the other hand, worries not a little about our faith in his ability to vindicate and to save.

The concerns of both God and people are taught in this parable of the persistent widow. Luke tells us at the outset that Jesus told this parable to people who were no longer praying because they had lost heart (v. 1). Then in a climactic line at the end of the parable Jesus poses the question in the mind of God: "When the Son of Man comes, will he find faith on earth?" (v. 8).

Luke skillfully ties this parable in with what he reported earlier. The Pharisees had asked Jesus when the kingdom of God was coming (17:20). People, you see, were waiting for God's kingdom to come, for God's glorious reign over a troubled earth, for deliverance from Roman oppression, for some an otherworldly heaven perhaps, and had not seen it. Funny thing they hadn't. It was there in front of them. Jesus tells them: "For . . . the kingdom of God is among you" (17:21). Jesus goes on to say that the day will come when people will desire to see "one of the days of the Son of Man," but they will not see it (17:22).

The Pharisees were then reminded of the story of Noah (17:26) in which people ate, drank, and were merry while Noah built his ark. Probably also for a short while after. Noah heard the Lord's word in faith, and with his family and the animals he entered the ark. The door was closed, and the time for hearing God's word and refraining from violence was past. The rains came and covered the earth.

"When the Son of Man Comes, Will He Find Faith?"

Something similar happened when God decreed judgment upon the wicked cities of Sodom and Gomorrah (17:28). On that occasion Lot and his family had to be dragged out of the city. Lot's sons-in-law laughed at the divine messengers, and stayed behind; Lot's wife never made it to safety. Well might God be concerned, then, about individuals showing faith when he comes to judge evil, while at the same time wanting to redeem some.

Jesus could have cited other examples. I think of Jeremiah, who much of the time stood alone preaching the judging and saving word of God when most people had itching ears to hear someone tell them all was well. Jerusalem and all Judah was slated for destruction, but Jeremiah was promised deliverance if he would keep the faith and believe God's word.

Jeremiah did keep the faith, although not without a struggle. No other prophet is so honest in letting us in on his complaints to God, some of them near-blasphemous outcries. In one he called God a "dried-up brook" for not ministering to his brokenness (Jer 15:18). Had he forgotten his earlier preaching that God was "the fountain of living water" (2:13)? On that occasion God had to tell him to repent, which he presumably did. The promise of deliverance, given him at the time of his call, was then repeated if Jeremiah would keep the faith. And Jeremiah did keep the faith, being spared when Nebuchadnezzar and the Babylonians leveled Jerusalem and carried survivors into faraway exile. On another occasion Jeremiah cursed the day of his birth and the man who brought the happy news to his father, asking at the end of a pathos-filled confession why he was even born (20:14–18). The answer came in his call, when God said he was born because God called him before he was born to be a prophet to the nations (1:5).

In this dreadful time Jeremiah gave others a promise of deliverance. There was Baruch, his scribe and confidant, who came to the prophet and lamented over a lost career that would have brought him greatness. Jeremiah told him he should be happy to escape with his own life at such a time, when the nation was plunging headlong into ruin (Jer 45). Baruch was delivered, surviving the nation's destruction with Jeremiah and staying with him on the sojourn to Egypt.

And there was Ebed-melech, a black man employed as a domestic in King Zedekiah's palace, who rescued Jeremiah out of the pit. He too was promised deliverance in this terrible time (Jer 39:15–18). We may assume that he too survived, although Scripture does not tell us that he did.

Jesus tells the Pharisees it will be no different when he returns to wind up human history. He says, "I tell you, on that night there will be two in one bed; one will be taken and the other left. There will be two women grinding meal together; one will be taken and the other left." (Luke 17:34–36).

Jesus knew his generation had lost courage; it was without hope; it had no faith. To such a generation he tells the parable of the persistent widow and the unrighteous judge. The characters in the parable are somewhat exaggerated, but that is only to make a point. The judge is a very bad judge. He is so bad that he condemns himself saying, "Though I have no fear of God and no respect for anyone . . ." The widow, too, is frankly a pest, although we need not assume that her plea was a trivial one.

Widows were much oppressed in the ancient world. They were usually poor, most often because of debts they could not pay. The rich took advantage of them, sometimes seizing their last article of outer clothing as a pledge, even though Israelite law forbade it (Deut 24:17). Job censures those taking a widow's ox in pledge (Job 24:3), or worse yet, those who snatch an orphan child from its mother's breast and take in pledge infants of the poor (Job 24:9). The widow crying to the prophet Elisha says her husband died and the creditor had come to take away her two children to be his slaves (2 Kgs 4:1). When the Israelites affirmed the covenant at Shechem, the priest called out, "Cursed be anyone who deprives the alien, the orphan, and the widow of justice," and the people shouted a loud amen (Deut 27:19).

The woman in this parable undoubtedly had a legitimate claim to bring before the judge, and her persistence is a match for the judge's unwillingness to hear the case—a situation obtaining earlier in Jerusalem and observed by Jeremiah (Jer 5:28). But in the end justice is achieved. When one compares this judge with God, it is obvious there is a vast difference between them: God is a righteous judge, being much concerned about the pleas of the poor. In the Law it says, "If you take your neighbor's cloak in pawn, you shall restore it before the sun goes down; for it may be your neighbor's only clothing to use as a cover; in what else shall that person sleep? And if your neighbor cries out to me, I will listen, for I am compassionate" (Exod 22:26–27). God will certainly act for that person's vindication—particularly a widow who calls upon him. God will act quickly; he does not need to be pestered, although in prayer we often do just that.

The pesty widow is to be for us a mirror, even though God is probably wearied with pesty people such as we are. The point is that the widow possesses the one attribute we lack when injustice prevails, when our courage fails, when our hope is lost, and when faith is nonexistent or nearly so: She is relentless in her supplication. Jesus says, "Ask, and it will be given you;

"When the Son of Man Comes, Will He Find Faith?"

search, and you will find; knock, and the door will be opened for you" (Matt 7:7).

Scripture, it is true, places more emphasis on a God who has found us than on a God who needs to be sought out. But they are two sides to every coin. We must never forget the other great scriptural teaching, which is that God wants us to actively seek him, particularly when our hearts and minds are impure and we need cleansing, also pardon. You know the words well:

> Seek the Lord while he may be found
>   call upon him while he is near
> let the wicked forsake their way
>   and the unrighteous their thoughts
> let them return to the Lord, that he may have mercy on them
>   and to our God, for he will abundantly pardon
> (Isa 55:6–7)

This persistent widow is a lesson to all of us, who, when an injustice has been done to ourselves or another, sit on our hands and do nothing. We neither approach individuals acting in an unrighteous manner, nor do we pray to the God of all righteousness. Where is the courage of this persistent woman to approach people we do not want to approach, or to pray to God about things too sensitive or unpleasant? Where is the hope of this persistent woman that is never lost on eventual vindication regarding this matter or that? And where is this persistent woman's faith, which remains alive when the faith of all friends is probably gone—a faith that God will answer prayers and right the injustices facing us and those around us? The question is not whether God will act for our vindication and salvation. The question is rather the one Jesus asks at the end of the parable: "When the Son of Man comes, will he find faith on earth?"

We see today people marching in cities to alleviate world poverty, particularly in Africa. In Edinburgh, Scotland, where the G-8 is meeting, some two hundred thousand marched through the streets in the hopes of getting world leaders to do even more than they are doing to wipe out debts of those unable to pay them. But we should not overlook the fact that the G-8 has already done something to forgive debts in Africa.

Our God is a God of active grace, a God who aids the poor, feeds the hungry, delivers needy people in distress. Usually, when we come to our senses we find that he is already at work in our midst, and like the Pharisees we have simply been unable to see it. That is the meaning of "He will quickly grant justice to them" in v. 8.

What is required of Christians is active faith—a faith that shows itself in praying when we think it's not worth praying; a faith that tells others to pray when they think it's not worth it, or have quit praying altogether; a faith that shows itself in a hope that God—in his own time and in his own way—will right injustices we think will never be righted; a faith that shows itself in courage to do what we can about the problems in our world, in our families, and within ourselves, instead of turning a blind eye and doing nothing; a faith that shows itself in affirming God, the Lord Jesus, and the church, also working to correct the latter when enormous stupidities are being done in the name of all three, bringing embarrassment to other believers and compromising the faith before a world that looks on wondering if claims of the God we worship are real.

The real question, let us remember, is not whether God will come to vindicate and save us. God has already acted to save the world in Jesus Christ (John 3:16), a work that will be completed in a harvest God has slated for the end of time. The real question is this: When the Son of Man comes—now or later—will he find faith? AMEN

Stages of the Christian Walk

23

The Challenge of Young Adulthood: Intimacy or Isolation?[1]

Lent

Text: John 19:26–27

When Jesus saw his mother and the disciple whom he loved standing beside her, he said to his mother, "Woman, here is your son." Then he said to the disciple, "Here is your mother." And from that hour the disciple took her into his own home.

During the past forty years or so important work has been done in the study of human development. It began with Erik Erikson and his life-cycle theory, which was published in 1950. Erikson studied how the human person develops and came to the conclusion that there are eight basic stages from birth to old age. He tested his theory against the life of Martin Luther, and it has been applied broadly ever since. The eight stages—and issues characterizing them—are,

1) Infancy: Basic Trust and Basic Mistrust

2) Early Childhood: Autonomy vs. Shame and Doubt

---

1. Preached at the Beverly Covenant Church in Chicago, Illinois, on March 4, 1990.

3) Play Age: Initiative and Guilt

4) School Age: Industry vs. Inferiority

5) Adolescence: Identity vs. Identity Confusion

6) Young Adulthood: Intimacy vs. Isolation

7) Adulthood: Generativity vs. Stagnation

8) Mature Adulthood: Integrity vs. Despair and Disgust

According to Erikson, we work through these issues at key stages of our maturation—everyone does—and the extent to which we negotiate them successfully is the extent to which we become healthy individuals. Negotiating one stage prepares you for the next. For example, you have to learn to trust in infancy before you can become your own person in early childhood. Developing initiative during the Play Age makes possible industry in School Age, and so forth.

Also, it is very important that you end up with positive traits outweighing negative ones, strengths outweighing weaknesses. That is, you should end up trusting more than mistrusting; your strength of will should overcome your sense of shame and doubt; in old age integrity should dominate over despair and disgust.

At the same time so-called negative traits are not entirely done away with, which is very important. People must know when to mistrust; they must have some shame and doubt; they must feel guilt; they must feel inferior to someone; they must have some questions about who they are; some of the time they must be off by themselves.

As a matter of fact, too little of the negative traits will cause problems, just as too little of the positive traits will. Here it is possible to get stuck in a stage if too great an imbalance exists. For example, if one trusts or mistrusts too much during infancy, one can get stuck—or we might say hung up—on trust issues for the rest of life, saying too frequently, "Can I trust this person?" Or, "I don't trust him or her." Or, "You can't trust city hall," and so forth.

Today and during the coming Sundays I would like to focus on four basic struggles said to take place during adulthood. I do not mean to champion all of Erikson's ideas, nor posit stages quite as neat as his outline suggests. As a matter of fact, I will focus next week on a transition stage based on another study of human development. But I believe important things

The Challenge of Young Adulthood: Intimacy or Isolation?

are to be learned in this general area. Erikson's life-cycle theory is now being studied in our seminaries.

I am at the point where I would suggest that this be placed on a par—maybe even ahead—of evangelism on our agenda. Why? Because (1) many people in our churches lack common maturity enabling them to witness effectively; and (2) those much concerned about witness or busily engaged in witness are sorely lacking in Christian maturity, with the result that their witness fails or worse yet, they inflict long-term harm in the struggle to bring people to a genuine and mature faith in Jesus Christ. In either case, the results are disastrous. Witnessing for Christ is a sorry affair when one does not have his or her own life together, or when one has not matured in Jesus Christ.

This morning I want to focus on young adulthood, which I suppose covers roughly twenty to thirty, give or take a few years. According to Erikson, during this time we must develop intimate relationships with others; we must overcome a rising tendency within us to become isolated. The young adulthood stage builds on adolescence. During adolescence we struggle with our identity (i.e., who we are, the importance we have as a person, recognizing that in some mysterious way we are a self made up of many selves).

Friends assume great importance during adolescence, mostly in helping us to find out who we are. During the adolescent years children in a family come to realize that they are not one of their brothers or sisters, but someone entirely different, possessing a worth all their own. Erikson says this is the time when one develops a true consciousness of God. The two brothers in the parable of the lost (prodigal) son may be in this stage of development.

When you complete adolescence, you should know that you are a unique and special person, and be something you feel good about. Friends may go in another direction, but this does not worry you; you have your own path ahead of you, and it is a special path. During the late teens one often settles on a vocation, which helps reinforce one's sense of identity.

Now one must let go of any achievement so one can advance to the next stage, which is young adulthood. In young adulthood one struggles with intimacy versus isolation, and intimacy has to come out the victor. Success during this stage means nothing less than letting go of yourself in order that you may share yourself with others. Taking the step into marriage is the most obvious example of this stage occurring. Intimacy should also develop along healthy lines with people at work, with friends, with people at church, and so forth.

Individuals in early adulthood who withdraw into a world of their own are not negotiating this stage successfully. This is a disturbing feature in many young marriages, where husband and wife spend too much time doing their own thing. Some isolation, of course, is necessary and good, but isolation must not dominate. Life is to be shared. Marriages in which people do not grow together—what Erikson calls a "sharing of selves"—grow apart, and the end result is divorce, which I need not tell you has reached near-epidemic proportions in our society.

Only people who are secure in themselves can risk sharing their lives with others, for sharing means loss, or at least risking loss. Compromises—so necessary in achieving a strong marriage—are not possible without giving up something.

There is also the problem of self-esteem. People with low self-esteem cannot get close to others; they cannot really give themselves to others—because they are afraid. It is a frightful thing when others find out we have pockets of emptiness.

Missionaries must be secure in themselves if they hope to develop intimacies necessary in reaching people for Christ. Missionary activity, more than any other activity in the church, risks loss, and missionaries must be secure in knowing that they themselves are a child of God before venturing out to bring others into God's family.

I'd like for us now to have a look into the Old Testament where we have a good example of someone who did not negotiate the struggle of young adulthood very well. That individual was King Saul. You see it right off when the people want to elect him king how little self-esteem he has. After his name is chosen, he is nowhere to be found. Someone finally discovers him hiding among the baggage (1 Sam 10:22).

This seems a bit funny, but Saul's low self-esteem is not funny. Samuel saw it as an unhealthy trait when he berated Saul for disobeying the Lord's command. He said to Saul: "Though you are little in your own eyes, are you not the head of the tribes of Israel?" (1 Sam 15:17).

Do not mistake an inferiority complex with humility; it is just the opposite. It indicates too much ego, the excess being an embarrassment one tries to hide by pretending to be unimportant. We are taught that true humility is not thinking more of ourselves than we ought to think, which

The Challenge of Young Adulthood: Intimacy or Isolation?

is true. But true humility is also thinking enough of ourselves to affirm our worth.

Saul shows that he has not successfully negotiated the adolescence stage in that he doesn't know his limits, which among the Greeks would cast him as a tragic figure. Saul and also his son Jonathan have a problem with disobedience. On one occasion it nearly costs Jonathan his life (1 Sam 14:36–45), and it does cost Saul the kingship (1 Sam 15:22–23).

Saul also has not developed sufficient identity during his adolescence, which leads to failure in the intimacy stage. He lacks real intimacy with Samuel, and he lacks it with also with David, which shows itself later. Saul at first is very partial to David, but as soon as he fears David might replace him, he becomes hostile and tries to kill him. In his older years Saul becomes increasingly isolated, and at the end of life is an intensely lonely man. The Spirit of the Lord is said to have left him, replaced, the Bible says, by an evil spirit of the Lord that tormented him the rest of his days (1 Sam 16:14). Saul's isolation ended in suicide, to which was added the indignity of having his body and the bodies of his sons impaled on the walls of Bethshan by the Philistines (1 Sam 31). Isolation won out over intimacy in the life of Israel's first king.

In contrast to the tragic figure of Saul is Jesus, who successfully negotiated all crises in human life. The crisis of young adulthood was no exception. Because Jesus knew who he was, he was capable of intimacy with others. More than that, he could and did cultivate intimacy between others. Jesus' struggle during the forty days in the wilderness tested the certainty of his identity, climaxed surely in his baptism by John. Jesus knows his limits: e.g., he does not try to turn stones into bread or jump off the temple roof. Jesus is also obedient—throughout life and at the end of life—in a way Saul was not.

We see intimacy prevailing over isolation in Jesus' relation with the twelve. Not one is a threat to him. At one point his followers were all about to leave him, but he simply asked the twelve, "Do you also wish to go away?" (John 6:67). Jesus shared himself with his disciples in a way no other person did, and as a result they were fulfilled and brought to greater maturity.

On the cross, in a moment of agonizing isolation, we see Jesus rising above his own isolation to form shared identities with others. He entrusts his mother to the beloved disciple, and the beloved disciple to his mother. The importance of both to him cannot be overestimated. Jesus was not thinking of himself and how his loss would devastate others. That is what a person contemplating suicide thinks. Rather he affirms precious intimacy of prior times, and proposes an expanded intimacy between his mother and the beloved disciple in days ahead.

Jesus is so secure in his moment of death that he can give himself up to God and let go of two very dear persons in life, while the soldiers toss dice to see who will take his robe. It is not that he did not feel isolated. He did. His cry with words from the beginning of Psalm 22 shows profound isolation. But the point is that isolation does not prevail; it comes not even close to winning out in what has to be the loneliest experience for anyone at any time.

What won out in the end was intimacy, and we are the beneficiaries, because what was happening on the cross was that Jesus made atonement—at-one-ment—between God and a whole world tragically isolated from him. AMEN

24

The Challenge of Midlife Transition: Creation or Destruction?[1]

Text: Romans 6:4

Therefore we have been buried with him by baptism into death, so that, just as Christ was raised from the dead by the glory of the Father, we too might walk in newness of life.

Last week I spoke about intimacy and isolation as being the preeminent struggle occurring in young adulthood according to sociologist Erik Erikson. Next week I will pick up on Erikson's description of middle adulthood, but today I want to focus on one of the important transitions adults are expected to make. It is the so-called midlife transition.

Here I am indebted to the work of Yale psychologist Daniel Levinson, who has written a best-selling book titled *The Seasons of a Man's Life*. It was this book that inspired Gail Sheehy to write *Passages*, a more popular book perhaps some of you have read. If there are important stages (or seasons) in a person's life, there are also important transitions as one moves from one stage to another. Transitions are important not only for what happens in human development, but for the evaluation we make of them.

Levinson devoted attention to the midlife transition, which is said to take place roughly between the ages of forty and forty-five. It can begin at thirty-eight and go to forty-seven, says Levinson, but with most people it is beginning by forty and over by forty-five. Long before Levinson's research

---

1. Preached at the Beverly Covenant Church in Chicago, Illinois, on March 18, 1990

people were conscious of something significant happening about this time. People with a positive outlook would say, "Life begins at forty." Others—perhaps just as many—would not admit to having had their fortieth birthday. They were eternally thirty-nine.

Why all the to-do about reaching forty? Levinson says that at forty, one knows more than ever before that one is going to die. You can feel it in your bones, in your dreams, in the marrow of your being. Death is no longer an abstract notion; it is something concrete and real. Before, you knew that flowers, trees, animals, and other people died; but now you know you will die. Another thirty years no longer seem that long. More years may lie behind you than lie ahead. You realize that you have become the dominant generation, but at the same time you know this is but a temporary thing.

The awareness that we are going to die is painful, and it heightens within us feelings of destructiveness—deep feelings of destructiveness. They are commonly of three types: First, we come to realize that we have done destructive things to others. Some were unavoidable, but some were not. If we do not come to this realization on our own, others will tell us. Second, we come to realize that others have done destructive things to us, and we hurt, and may also be angry. Thirdly, we become overwhelmed by destructive forces in our world. We may think "everything is going to hell."

John Milton lived in seventeenth century England during a period of great social change. Blinded at the age of forty-two, having suffered severe misfortunes in his personal life, being dedicated to a lawful social order, believing in a just God, and enraged at the injustices being perpetuated in God's world, he gives us a glimpse into his midlife struggle in these lines from *Paradise Lost*:

> Which way shall I fly
> Infinite wrath and infinite despair?
> Which way I fly is hell; myself am hell
> And in the lowest deep a lower deep
> Still threat'ning to devour me, opens wide
> To which the hell I suffer seems a heaven

Our sense of mortality and preoccupation with destruction can affect us in other ways. We can create the illusion that mortality and destruction do not exist, or become so overwhelmed by our anxiety, guilt, and grievances against others that we become frozen, as it were, living, but not really living. But we can also become creative, more creative than ever before.

The Challenge of Midlife Transition: Creation or Destruction?

This is the challenge of the midlife transition: creation or destruction? Do we give in to destructive urges resident within us, acquiesce to the destruction going on around us, or do we become creative, venturing out into new things, doing what we barely thought possible, and living life so it really begins to add up to something?

Levinson finds people becoming really creative at this time in life—some people that is. For them life does begin at forty, whereas being a perpetual thirty-nine adds up to a tragic admission that one is giving in to forces of destruction. One way of not experiencing a creative burst in life is to become what's called a pretender. We can pretend we have not hurt others; we can pretend not to have been hurt by others; we can pretend things are not that bad out in the world, at home, in our families, or in other worlds we inhabit—including the church. Pretenders are prevented from loving and affirming life; they are prevented from being creative at a time when they have the greatest opportunity to be creative.

In living by illusion, we fool ourselves, and at times manage to fool others. By not admitting our guilt, not admitting our hurt, not expressing our frustration about the world we allow all these bothersome things to continue, which leaves us part of the problem, instead of part of the solution. It makes our life less and less real.

It is equally bad when we become overwhelmed by our hurts, our guilt, and our despair of the world. We need a healthy amount of each, as I said last week about negative polarities in the struggles of human development. But they need to be controlled; they cannot take over. If they do, it will happen again that we become part of the problem instead of part of its solution, and life will become less and less real life.

The way to creativity for the believer is the way of God's leading. We find this in the Old Testament where persons of faith time and again overcome destructive forces of enormous proportions to be creative, affirm life, and discover hope—not only for themselves but a hope they can pass on to others.

The story of Joseph is a grand story of creation winning out over destruction. God, of course, is the prime mover of events, as the Bible tells the story, and to what extent Joseph had creative tendencies of his own, or survived his midlife transition, we cannot say. But at the end of his life Joseph gives one little window into himself where it becomes clear that creation has won out over destruction. He tells his brothers in that unforgettable encounter: "As for you, you meant evil against me; but God meant it for good, to bring it about that many people should be kept alive, as they are today" (Gen 50:20).

This is not someone who gave in to destructive forces, which seemed only to accumulate early in life—being sold into slavery by his brothers, being unjustly accused of wrongdoing with Potiphar's wife, being unjustly sent to prison and then left there by another unfortunate turn of events. Any one of these experiences would have been enough to make him wish he were dead.

I think too of Jeremiah, who lived during a most destructive time when Jewish nationhood came spiraling to an end. We open his book and are immediately struck with the destructive tone of the prophet's message. I spoke some time ago about Jeremiah to a women's Bible class, and one of the ladies asked me how I could stand so much talk about sin, suffering, and destruction. Already she had had enough. I told her the question had been put to me before. I knew what she was talking about. I gave her an answer, but before doing so I confided to her that I usually do not let Bible studies in Jeremiah go very long. Few can stand the ongoing message in this book.

But—and this is important—we get from this prophet some of the most incredible creative impulses ever unleashed. Because of all the doom preaching, the persecutions, and brutally frank complaints to God, many have failed to discover the creative Jeremiah. Jeremiah lives out his entire life believing the promise that God will save him, even though most everyone else will die or be taken into exile. And in chapters 30–31 Jeremiah has some very upbeat oracles about a reunion of north and south and the return to Zion—second only to Second Isaiah (Isa 40–55) in inspiration and power.

When Jerusalem is about to be taken by the Babylonians, Jeremiah buys property in his home village of Anathoth as a sign that people will one day return to inhabit the land—an act, on the face of it, that is pure foolishness (Jer 32:6–12). Land is usually a good investment, but not in war because you can't take it with you. But Jeremiah buys land on the eve of Jerusalem's destruction. About this same time Jeremiah gives us lofty words about a new covenant (here called an eternal or everlasting covenant) that becomes a virtual charter for the Christian church (Jer 32:36–44). Is this a prophet simply fixated on a message of destruction? I submit to you that what we see in Jeremiah is a life controlled not by destructive forces—even though it had every reason to be—but one controlled by God-given

The Challenge of Midlife Transition: Creation or Destruction?

messages of faith and hope. Creation won out in the life of Jeremiah, not destruction!

For the apostle Paul, the way to creativity lay in Christian baptism. In baptism one comes to terms with the death of Jesus, with one's sin, with one's death that is a consequence of sin, and finally with the grace of God through which the baptized person is given newness of life. Baptism, of course, could come at forty, and for some it does or at another time in mature adulthood, but for the majority of Christians it takes place early in life. However and whenever it happens, baptism is a real dying with Jesus (which in immersion is what going under the water symbolizes), and a real creation of new life (which is what coming up out of the water symbolizes). In baptism we affirm the creative power of God—today and in days to come.

For those of us who have died and risen with Christ, we live or should live above the sins of destruction, knowing we have been freed from them and any guilt about them. We live above and beyond destruction others have done to us, knowing that in the economy of God these things will go nowhere, or otherwise are turned by God into something good. We rise above destruction in our world, first by accepting it, and second by doing something creative to help eliminate it.

Is God doing a work of creation in you this morning? Or are you doing your own work of destruction? Is anything in your life creative? Have you a "cutting edge"? Are you transforming evil into good, useless things into useful things, and seeing what is dead or left for dead becoming something wondrously alive? Can you sing new songs? Can you enjoy changes in life, changes in yourself, and changes in the worship of God?

The death and resurrection of Jesus is to give us newness of life, which is the Bible's way of talking about creation. We dare not affirm anything less in the Christian walk, for to do so is to rob the gospel of its power. AMEN

25

The Challenge of Adulthood: Generativity or Stagnation?[1]

Text: Matthew 25:14–30

For it is as if a man, going on a journey, summoned his slaves and entrusted his property to them; to one he gave five talents, to another two, to another one, to each according to his ability. Then he went away. The one who had received the five talents went off at once and traded with them, and made five more talents. In the same way, the one who had the two talents made two more talents. But the one who had received the one talent went off and dug a hole in the ground and hid his master's money. After a long time the master of those slaves came and settled accounts with them. Then the one who had received the five talents came forward, bringing five more talents, saying, "Master, you handed over to me five talents; see, I have made five more talents." His master said to him, "Well done, good and trustworthy slave; you have been trustworthy in a few things, I will put you in charge of many things; enter into the joy of your master." And the one with the two talents also came forward, saying, "Master, you handed over to me two talents; see, I have made two more talents." His master said to him, "Well done, good and trustworthy slave; you have been trustworthy in a few things, I will put you in charge of many things; enter into the joy of your master." Then the one who had received the one talent also came forward, saying, "Master, I knew that you were a harsh man, reaping where you did not sow, and gathering where you did not scatter seed; so I was afraid, and I went and hid your talent in the ground.

---

1. Preached at the Beverly Covenant Church in Chicago, Illinois, on March 25, 1990.

The Challenge of Adulthood: Generativity or Stagnation?

Here you have what is yours." But his master replied, "You wicked and lazy slave! You knew, did you, that I reap where I did not sow, and gather where I did not scatter? Then you ought to have invested my money with the bankers, and on my return I would have received what was my own with interest. So take the talent from him, and give it to the one with the ten talents. For to all those who have, more will be given, and they will have an abundance; but from those who have nothing, even what they have will be taken away. As for this worthless slave, throw him into the outer darkness, where there will be weeping and gnashing of teeth.

Earlier in this Lenten series I spoke about the struggle in the teen years to become our own person, and about how as young adults we work at becoming truly intimate—with one other person typically, but to a lesser extent also with other people.

You perhaps have noticed that maturity, according to this line of thinking, is a gradual move away from self-centeredness. The first cautious step away from thinking that we are at the "top of the world," or at the "center of the world," is a move to share our identities with the identities of others. Mature adulthood involves this important step in the socialization process: we move away from ourselves in the direction of others. It has important applications to the life of faith and our life before God.

Middle adulthood is broadly defined as the years between thirty and fifty, or twenty-five and fifty-five. Because Erik Erikson worked more with childhood, his stages in this area were more precise than later stages. So limits here are not that precise. It is perhaps just as well. All we need to know is that in middle adulthood we are not yet into old age.

The struggle people experience in middle adulthood, according to Erikson, has to do with "generativity," i.e., the task of generating life. In its basic and most obvious form it consists of having children. In our younger years we are like cars on a train; now what is required of us is that we become the engine. In middle adulthood we are asked to show that some power is at work within us. Are we pulling other cars? Have we taken responsibility for guiding the next generation? The most obvious form of generativity, as I say, is raising children. If life is to move forward, we must nurture and inspire the generation following so it can carry on after us.

The opposite response to the challenge of middle adulthood is what Erikson calls "stagnation," which means pretty much what it says. A person who remains stagnant is either sitting still or continuing to be pulled along by others. There are those who never themselves become engines. Others look to be engines but do not have the power switch on. And still others are engines making a loud roar but going nowhere because they are not in gear. In stagnation energy is lacking or energy is being used up on ourselves. Stagnant people are absorbed in themselves and what they are doing; they are negligent in child-rearing; they are negligent or unwilling to help others in need; they are people without life in God and in Jesus Christ.

There is a shocking amount of stagnation today in child-rearing. It takes time and energy to parent children, particularly demanding or difficult children. Too often the job simply does not get done. Children cannot raise themselves, whatever you may think. They need someone to talk to when they come home from school—about things important to them in their day; they need someone who will listen, someone who will share their thoughts on this matter or that, and someone who will advise; they need a mother and father who will teach them skills learned so they too can be productive, find out what brings success in life, and what dangers they need to watch out for in order to keep trouble away (read the book of Proverbs in the Old Testament). What children do not need today is more television, which, besides the problem of bad programming, is the problem of a medium that leaves children too passive!

If we as adults fail to generate—whether it be with our own children or with the other young people around us—we will become forgotten and unappreciated in old age, selfishness yielding two of its bitter fruits. A China missionary, Edla Matson, paid special attention to me as a young boy, and I remain eternally grateful to this dear woman, for in a small but significant way she helped me become the person I am today. There were others, and you, too, know of people in your growing up years who had generative power with you.

In the Old Testament we see someone who was very energetic in his youth, but in old age appears to have failed when it came to generativity. I refer to David, king of Israel, who seemed unable to decide who would succeed him. He needed help from Bathsheba (1 Kgs 1:15–31). That David had many fine qualities goes without saying, and that he became a model for Jesus and his messianic work is clear from the New Testament, but this should not blind us to what the biblical writer goes to great lengths to tell us, namely, that this great man was sorely deficient as a father, to the point that it nearly cost him the kingship.

The Challenge of Adulthood: Generativity or Stagnation?

We get more than a hint of David's self-centeredness as an adult when he takes—actually steals—the wife of his valued servant, Uriah the Hittite. Stagnation appears to have set in about this time. Hear the words of the biblical writer introducing the Bathsheba affair:

> In the spring of the year, the time when kings go out to battle, David sent Joab with his officers and all Israel with him; they ravaged the Ammonites, and besieged Rabbah. *But David remained at Jerusalem.* (2 Sam 11:1)

Immediately after began problems with his sons (2 Samuel 13). First it was Amnon, who raped his sister Tamar. When David heard about it, he became angry but did nothing.

Sitting still is what stagnation is all about. David's son Absalom, however, did not sit still. Because David sat still nothing was resolved, so Absalom rose up and killed Amnon. Again David is grieved but doesn't know what to do. Absalom runs away. David is hurt by his absence, but won't do anything to get him to come home.

The king needs help, which is forthcoming from his commander Joab. Joab has to trick David to get the king's consent to bring Absalom back, but it works, and Absalom is returned to Jerusalem. But not to see his father. David wants him out of his presence, so Absalom remains in a separate house. How long is it possible to keep a child in his room or somewhere separate from parents who remain angry? Absalom lives alone two years without seeing his father.

Absalom wants to see David, and sends messages via Joab to that effect, but these are disregarded. Finally, to get Joab's attention Absalom sets fire to Joab's field of barley. This gets his attention. Absalom finally gets to see his father.

If you wonder why young people do radical things, why children have temper tantrums on the floor, why radical students in the 1960s brought universities and other institutions to a halt, why people in all ages resort to violent behavior, leaving people dead and property destroyed, the answer is often that they have been ignored beyond limit. You say they are self-centered. Yes, perhaps. But those against whom they strike out are also self-centered, sometimes more so.

The Absalom story gets worse. A rebellion is organized and Absalom sets out to kill his father. He nearly succeeds. David is forced to flee Jerusalem and only after Joab and the army kill Absalom is he able to return safely to the city. Succession to the throne is resolved finally when Solomon is proclaimed king, but again David needs help, this time from his wife to keep Adonijah from becoming king after having already been crowned by a group of loyalists (1 Kings 1–2).

For all of David's good qualities he lacks the power of generativity. He fails to be the engine needed to bring the next generation along. David's middle adulthood is plagued with stagnation. After having won all his battles, he now sits back to relax as if his work as king and father is all done.

From the New Testament we also learn something about generativity. In the parable of the talents Jesus tells us that the kingdom of heaven is like money needing investment so it can earn on the principal. The servants winning praise are those who invest wisely and bring the master a return. The servant who buried his money in the ground gets severe judgment. What is more, the money he was given now goes to the one who already has a lot.

Talents are money, but the message of this parable is not ultimately about money and investing it, for which reason talents have commonly been broadened to mean an array of the gifts we possess. This is fine. The point of the parable is that Christians must take whatever God gives them and generate more. We must broaden its application more to include the young people entrusted to us—children and other young people from whom God expects one day a yield.

Generativity, I hasten to say, is not motivation. According to the motivation experts it is not possible to motivate others. Motivation is something within a person, and if there is a switch to be turned on, it is an inner switch that can only be turned on by the person themself; it cannot be turned on from outside. Generativity, however, is energy expended to carry others along with you.

How does this happen? That is a more vexing question and may in the end remain a mystery. But in the life of faith pointers found in Scripture and in traditions handed down in the church can help us formulate an answer. I would mention just four: (a) by teaching, (b) by example, (c) by prayer, and (d) by nurture and fellowship available in the church.

We bring children into this world and provide them with food and countless toys. But this is scarcely enough. We must teach them about life; we must teach them to love God and honor our Lord Jesus; we must teach them the faith others taught us; and in light of these teachings, we must talk over with them the struggles in their lives, the problems they have at school, yes, their boyfriends and girlfriends if they are willing to talk about them.

More important than all the teaching in the world is being a good example. One of the most serious problems in the church today is people who talk big and live small. We need to turn this around by talking small and living big; by rising to or above the principles we espouse, not living below them; by expecting more of ourselves and less of others.

Rabbi Gamaliel, grandson of the great Hillel and teacher of Paul (Acts 22:3; cf. 5:34–39), is reported to have said the following: "If a person's teachings are greater than his deeds, his teachings—no matter how good—will be forgotten; but if a person's deeds are greater than his teachings, his teachings—even though not outstanding—will be remembered."

Humility before God requires also that we pray for those coming under our charge, and that we pray too for ourselves, asking that God will give us more wisdom, more patience, more listening power, and more compassion than we presently have. Also, we should pray for other adults to enter into the lives of young people, not least of all our children. They can do what we cannot do. It is pure arrogance to think we can do it all, that the judgments of others are never as good as our own, that a different slant coming from someone else will only complicate things. Often a different slant is precisely what our young people need.

Here it helps to have grandparents around. Often they will give the young person a slant different from one given by the parents. During the turbulent '60s, in families and in churches, young people often found common cause with grandparents and others of this generation, getting from them a slant different from parents with whom they could not communicate.

This brings me to say a final word about the church. What better place is there to teach our young people, to be an example for them, to pray for them and with them, and to experience with them life-giving fellowship? The church in a very concrete sense is the body of Christ (Luther). In the church our young people have an unparalleled opportunity to mature as persons, and even more important, to mature as men and women walking with Jesus Christ.

May we invest in the human treasures God has given us, so that one day our investment can show a double or even greater return, and we can enter into the joy of our Master! AMEN

26

The Challenge of Mature Adulthood: Integrity or Despair?[1]

Palm Sunday

Text: Matthew 21:15–16

But when the chief priests and the scribes saw the amazing things that he did, and heard the children crying out in the temple, "Hosanna to the Son of David," they became angry and said to him, "Do you hear what these are saying?" Jesus said to them, "Yes; have you never read, 'Out of the mouths of infants and nursing babies you have prepared praise for yourself?'"

Mature adulthood contains one overriding challenge, according to Erik Erikson, and that is whether one comes to be controlled by a sense of integrity or despair. This challenge is said to come with all its force in the years from fifty-five on. At this age death is no longer far distant. We said that at forty, one comes to realize that more time may lie behind than what lies ahead. Now, the imbalance is no longer in doubt. One's life is pretty much a matter of record. It is difficult—maybe even impossible—to make a new beginning. Life must now be faced with a sense of integrity.

---

1. Preached at the Beverly Covenant Church in Chicago, Illinois, on April 8, 1990.

The Challenge of Mature Adulthood: Integrity or Despair?

What is meant by integrity? The dictionary says *integrity* is a basic soundness or wholeness. Integrity contains a strong element of honesty. When Erikson speaks about integrity, he has two things in mind: (1) an acceptance of the one and only life we have lived, and (2) a willingness to get in line with people of other generations, to join the march, so to speak, knowing we have a place in it.

First, the acceptance of our one and only life. A person who has integrity says, "My life counts for something; I am willing to own up to it good and bad, and I do not wish I had lived another." One need not endorse everything one has done, but one does have to say an overall yes to one's life. Included in this is an acceptance of others who have been significant in our life. We come to affirm these people. As Christians, we thank God for them. Such people would be teachers, neighbors, special aunts or uncles, grandparents, and friends. Most important is what Erikson calls a "new and different love for one's parents."

It takes a certain level of maturity to stop complaining about what our parents failed to do for us, what our teachers failed to do, what our brother or sister failed to do, what some people in the church failed to do. We can recognize faults in all of these, but the faults must no longer be huge roadblocks that keep us from traveling life's road to conclusion and fulfillment. Immaturity blames other people too much for failures we have experienced in life.

This stage has some interesting connections with other stages. In the teen years we discovered our self-identity; now we endorse and take responsibility for who we are. In young adulthood we learned to divide the focus between ourself and others; now we return to take an honest look at our own life, being at the same time honest enough to affirm others—faults and all.

This second characteristic of the integrity stage, namely, joining the march of generations, is the result of affirming our own life. We are not afraid, for example, of accepting a job we thought earlier we could not fill because previous holders were more qualified than we. When we decide to join the march of the generations, we show we are basically not afraid to die. Fear of death indicates despair, the other mood or force vying to take control in later adulthood.

Despair is common in old age; actually it descends upon many before old age, but because old age brings with it a breakdown of the defenses that conceal what is going on inside, despair surfaces or is more transparent in old age. Despair is when people cannot say yes to life. Despair is a cry that life has been bitter. Despair in its most extreme form may be an even deeper cry that one's life should not have been lived at all.

The wish never to have lived is old. Examples abound in classical literature, like the one from Euripides's *Daughters of Troy* (lines 634–637), where Andromache says,

> Mother, O mother, a fairer, truer word
> Hear, that I may with solace touch thine heart;—
> To have been unborn I count as one with death
> But better death than life in bitterness.[2]

On a somewhat lighter side was a record we played on the Victrola at our summer cottage dating from the 1920s, titled "I Wish I Had Died in My Cradle." The chorus went:

> I wish I had never seen sunshine
> I wish I had never seen rain
> I wish that your soul had not been my goal
> A prize that I sought all in vain
> I only wish someone had told me
> The love that you gave was untrue
> And I wish I had died in my cradle
> Before I grew up to love you.

In some people we see disgust, says Erikson, which is merely a hidden form of despair. By acting disgusted people make light of what really amounts to deep grief.

Like all the other struggles, this one too must have some of each component. Life cannot be lived without some disgust or despair. We would not be human if were it not so. But the point again is that the negative force cannot control us. To possess integrity we must live above and beyond our despair, affirming both our life and the lives of others.

Jeremiah, in my view, is the great prophet of integrity. Living during a most disturbing time, he preached to people who did not want to listen, pled with a people unwilling to give up evil ways, living on despite ridicule, persecution, and threats on his life; yet, at the moment of Jerusalem's destruction he is able to speak hope for the nation's future.

---

2. Arthur S. Way, trans. *The Tragedies of Euripides in English Verse*, vol. 2 (3 vols; London: Macmillan, 1896), 146.

The Challenge of Mature Adulthood: Integrity or Despair?

Jeremiah does plummet into despair—indeed he does—cursing the day he was born and the man who brought the joyful news to his father. His question at the end of chapter 20 is, "Why did I come forth from the womb, to see toil and sorrow and end my days in shame?" (v. 18 AB). But this word was not a final word. The first edition of the Jeremiah book appears to be chapters 1–20, and the compiler, in good rhetorical style, answers the prophet's cry with a word that came to him as a young boy, when the Lord said: "Before I formed you in the belly I knew you, and before you came forth from the womb I consecrated you, a prophet to the nations I appointed you" (Jer 1:5 AB). The Lord's first word to Jeremiah is the answer to his cry of despair. Jeremiah was born, the scribe tells us, because the Lord called him before he was born. Despair does not control Jeremiah; what controls him is integrity—integrity before God and integrity before people in his nation who were watching him closely.

Job makes a similar cry of despair, asking God why he was born, but here, too, the outburst does not become the controlling force amidst suffering. Job's life—which works out differently—is controlled by an unswerving integrity, as the conclusion to his book makes plain (Job 42).

Returning to Jeremiah, after the prophet gives his unforgettable temple oracles of 609 BC, we witness another great moment when court is called into session and Jeremiah is put on trial for his life. The good prophet's defense is simply, "It is the LORD who sent me to prophesy against this house and this city all the words you have heard" (Jer 26:12), which shows integrity, honesty, and soundness of character. And wonder of wonders, the words call forth integrity from those who hear them—officials in government and elders who rise up to defend him. One official, Ahikam, helped save Jeremiah from King Jehoiakim's wrath (26:24). The prophet was not put to death.

Jeremiah's integrity is perhaps most strongly attested to by biographical narrative in the book, which views him up close during Jerusalem's last days. No prophet is looked at so closely as Jeremiah. At the final days we are no longer listening to the prophet's preaching; rather we are viewing the man himself—his suffering, his pain, his obedience to the divine call. We witness a message being lived out in a whole person. From the time of the temple oracles to Jerusalem's fall, Jeremiah is between forty-three and fifty-three years of age, approaching mature adulthood.

Jesus is not even forty-three when he rides into Jerusalem, but the end of his life is approaching, and he knows it. As with Jeremiah, so also with

Jesus—teaching and miracles give way to a life of suffering being lived out, and we cannot take our eyes off him. The focus is now on the man himself. John begins narrating the passion in chapter 11 of his Gospel, roughly the middle of the book. Why? Because Jesus' last days convey a message lived out in the whole person.

Palm Sunday is another grand moment of truth—for Jesus and for Jerusalem. When we see him riding into the city, we are looking at a man living out in his whole being everything he has done and will do. There is not a hint of despair. Yes, he will later weep over the city; he will struggle prayerfully in the Garden; he will cry out on the cross. But on this day he rides with the confidence of one who knows and believes everything his life stands for. Does it not move you?

This great man of integrity marches into the temple and calls it a "den of robbers," turning over tables of moneychangers, after which he heals some who are lame and blind. The response of some present makes it clear that this is indeed a moment of truth. The chief priests and scribes are indignant. They are afraid. Jesus has stirred up their insecurity. But listen to the children. They are crying, "Hosanna to the Son of David."

Let us not too quickly pass by the children. Erikson makes an important observation about the way children respond to adults possessing integrity. He says, "Healthy children will not fear life if their elders have integrity enough not to fear death." Jesus did not fear death. Others standing by seem not to fear death. Therefore the children are unafraid—unafraid to live, to sing in loud voices, to praise God in this deeply troubled time.

There is an important tie-in between trust, which develops early in life, and integrity, which flowers later—a tie-in that binds generations together. Adults living with integrity inspire trust in small children. We must never forget this.

How does Jesus' ride into Jerusalem affect you this morning? You know what lies ahead: persecution, suffering, and death. Can you allow the children to cry out? Can you let their hosannas ring? Would you, if you could, throw your garment or palm branch on the road before him? Or would the dark cloud on the horizon stir up feelings of disgust or despair? Do you wonder why we rejoice today when so much suffering and agony lies ahead? In some church traditions the joy of Palm Sunday is totally lost in worship and sermons anticipating the passion.

If children and others around us are to be brought to a genuine trust in Jesus, we who claim the faith must live with integrity. Doing so, we ought

The Challenge of Mature Adulthood: Integrity or Despair?

on this day join with those who waved and sang when they saw their King ride into the city. What lies ahead is not only suffering and death, but a glorious resurrection, which anticipates the day about which John speaks in Revelation. He reports having seen

> a great multitude, that no one could count, from every nation, from all tribes and peoples and languages, standing before the throne and before the Lamb, robed in white, with palm branches in their hands. They cried out in a loud voice, saying "Salvation belongs to our God who is seated on the throne, and to the Lamb!"

Those standing around the throne are singing:

> Amen! Blessing and glory and wisdom
> and thanksgiving and honor
> and power and might
> be to our God for ever and ever!
> Amen (Rev 7:9–10, 12).

27

Reflecting the Glory[1]

Text: 2 Corinthians 3:18:

And all of us, with unveiled faces, seeing the glory of the Lord as though reflected in a mirror, are being transformed into the same image from one degree of glory to another; for this comes from the Lord, the Spirit.

Sanctify us in the truth; O God, your word is truth.

The book of Exodus reports that when Moses came down from Mount Sinai with the tablets of law his face was aglow after talking with God. Moses did not know it, but brother Aaron and the people did, and they were afraid to approach him. Finally they dared to come near. While he spoke and gave them God's law, his face continued to glow. By now Moses must have been told about it, for when he finished speaking he put a veil on his face (Exod 34:29–35).

Brightness radiating from a divinity has parallels in the ancient world. In Mesopotamia people believed a brightness shined from faces of the gods, a radiance shared also by royalty. Two ancient poems in the Bible speak about radiated brightness from the God of Israel. One appears in the book of Habakkuk, where it says:

---

1. Preached at St. Mark's Church, Sydney, Australia, on February 14, 2010.

> God came from Teman
>> the Holy One from Mount Paran
> His glory covered the heavens
>> and the earth was full of his praise
> The brightness was like the sun
>> rays came forth from his hand
>> where his power lay hidden.
>
> (Hab 3:3–4)

The other is the Blessing of Moses in Deuteronomy, where the prologue says this about Israel's God:

> Yahweh from Sinai came
>> and rose up from Seir for him.
> He shone forth from Mount Paran
>> and went from the thousands of holy ones
>> from his southland slopes for him.
>
> (Deut 33:2)

What took place in the desert became established practice, presumably throughout Moses's life. Moses would wear a veil while performing routine tasks, but when he entered the Tent of Meeting to speak with God, he would take the veil off. It would remain off while he addressed the people after emerging from the tent. But when he had finished, he would put the veil on again. This incident and subsequent practices are not mentioned again in the Old Testament.

This remarkable theophany becomes background for Jesus' transfiguration, which Matthew, Mark, and Luke all record. It may also lie behind John's interpretation of the crucifixion, where Jesus tells Nicodemus that the "Son of Man must be lifted up," enabling those who believe in him to be brought into the light (John 3:1–21). Paul cites the tradition about Moses in 2 Cor 3:4–18, giving it a new twist in developing his teaching on the old and new covenants.

The common thread running through all of these passages, viz., the reflected glory of God, is what I want to speak about this morning. It is an important biblical teaching about which we hear little or nothing today. The reflected glory of God is seen first on the face of Moses, then manifested preeminently in Jesus (who on a high mountain appears with a temporarily glorified Moses and Elijah), and is later bestowed upon all believers.

That the Exodus 34 passage has to do with reflected glory is recognized by the LXX, which translates v. 29: "Moses did not know that the appearance of the skin of his face *was glorified*" (δεδόξασται). The LXX and also the Jewish Targum are credited with interpreting this somewhat difficult Hebrew reading to mean that Moses had a "glowing face" when coming down from the mountain, not "horns" on his head. This latter interpretation comes from Jerome, who rendered the Hebrew *qâran* with the Latin *cornuta* ("it was horned"). In the Vulgate[2] Moses does not have a divine glow on his face but rather a face featuring a horn. Religious art in the Middle Ages carried on this tradition, the most famous portrayal being Michelangelo's *Moses* sculpture at San Pietro in Rome, in which Moses has two horns on his head. Nevertheless, it is now generally agreed that the reference in Exodus is to radiating skin on Moses's face, not to horns on his head.

The context makes this clear. The focus on divine glory carries over from the previous chapter where Moses, after being told he enjoys the Lord's favor, asks to see the Lord's "glory" (Exod 33:18). He wants a look at God's "face." But God has a limit to divine favor: Moses cannot see God's face. No one can see the face of God and live, for the divine glory—or brightness, since *glory* refers to brilliant light—is too much to behold.

This colorful biblical account concludes with the glory of the Lord passing by, and the Lord covering a safely positioned Moses with his hand. Moses sees only the Lord's back. What apparently happened, however, was that some of the Lord's glory attached itself to Moses, for when Moses entered the Tent of Meeting to talk with God, his face took on a divine glow. It goes without saying that Moses does not possess any glory of his own. The glory he possesses is a reflected glory—the glory of the Lord. Moses is neither a sun nor a star; he is a moon. Human "stars" are a modern phenomenon, and the search for them leads to Hollywood.

In the New Testament transfiguration account Elijah joins Moses in reflecting the glory of God. And why not? Elijah rode dramatically into heaven in a chariot, and in later Jewish tradition he is the prophet whose return will usher in the great day of the Lord (Mal 4:5–6). In Matthew and Mark the transfiguration is followed up by talk about Elijah's return, with Matthew reporting Jesus as saying that Elijah has already come in the person of John the Baptist (Matt 17:10–13).

So while the reflected glory of God is first seen on all three—Jesus, Moses, and Elijah—after the cloud comes and Jesus is named as God's "beloved son," the disciples look up to see Jesus only. Moses and Elijah are gone. Going down from the mountain, Jesus tells the disciples not to say anything

---

2. The Vulgate was translated by Saint Jerome.

about this until after he rises from the dead (Matt 17:9; Mark 9:9; Luke 9:21). In his resurrection Jesus will be glorified. Religious art frequently depicts Jesus with a halo around his head, which is to symbolize the glory he radiates. In the Eastern Church, icons also have halos around the heads of the saints, portraying their glory.

For Paul, the veil of unbelief is removed when one turns to the Lord Jesus. Believers with unveiled faces who have beheld the Lord's glory will be changed into the likeness of the Lord "from one degree of glory to another." An extraordinary statement, one further supported by what Paul goes on to tell the Corinthian church: "So if anyone is in Christ, there is a new creation; everything old has passed away, see, everything has become new" (2 Cor 5:17).

Again in the letter to the Ephesians Paul says:

> You were taught to put away your former way of life, your old self, corrupt and deluded by its lusts, and to be renewed in the spirit of your minds, and to clothe yourselves with the new self, created according to the likeness of God in true righteousness and holiness. (Eph 4:22–24)

I hear no clarion call today for Christians to show the reflected glory of God. Nor is attention given to this teaching in seminaries where I have been teaching. Apparently it is safer to teach and preach the assured sinful state of everyone: believers and unbelievers.

At the seminary where I taught last year a fellow was walking about in a shirt on the back of which was written, "Sin Boldly." (I checked the Web, and you can buy the shirt for ten dollars.) It might have helped had the shirt conveyed the whole of Luther's statement, which was made in a letter to Melanchthon from the Wartburg castle in 1521. He said, "Sin boldly, but believe more boldly still." I don't know what the fellow's intention was. I didn't ask him. It may have been too much to hear the apostle Paul telling believers that "they were being changed into [the Lord's] likeness from one degree of glory to another" (2 Cor 3:18).

I do not wish to be misunderstood. I am not advocating a doctrine of sanctification like those that have led people into grave error, and in the end have brought disillusionment and sorrow. However, it should be noted that we are hearing words about "going from one degree of glory to the other" from the same apostle who told the Roman church that "all have sinned and fall short of the glory of God" (Rom 3:23). And in the same letter Paul said, "We boast in our hope of sharing the glory of God" (Rom 5:2). It is the better part of wisdom to read the whole of Romans before claiming to know the mind of Paul. Elsewhere the New Testament, e.g., in Matthew's Sermon on the Mount, we are awakened to a higher righteousness expected of all those who follow Jesus.

It is a recurring New Testament theme that Christian believers are to reflect the glory of God, and that this reflected glory is to lead others to glorify God. Jesus says, "Let your light shine before others, so that they may see your good works and give glory to your Father in heaven" (Matt 5:16). Paul says, "So, whether you eat or drink, or whatever you do, do everything for the glory of God" (1 Cor 10:31). Again Paul tells the Corinthians, "For you were bought with a price; therefore glorify God in your body" (1 Cor 6:20); and to the Colossians he speaks of a great mystery, "Christ in you, the hope of glory" (Col 1:27).

The corollary to this is a warning throughout the Bible not to exchange the glory of God for inglorious behavior driven by false religion and worldly emptiness. Jeremiah says, "Has a nation changed its gods, even though they are no gods? But my people have changed their glory for something that does not profit" (Jer 2:11). From the psalmist is this word: "They made a calf at Horeb, and worshiped a cast image. They exchanged the glory of God for the image of an ox that eats grass" (Ps 106:19–20). And from Paul: "Claiming to become wise, they became fools; and they exchanged the glory of the immortal God for images resembling a mortal human being or birds or four-footed animals or reptiles" (Rom 1:22–23). Paul goes on to say that God has given up these misguided souls to the lusts of their hearts . . . and dishonorable passions (vv. 24–26). The litany of wickedness at the end of Romans 1 has uncomfortable echoes in our present world, unfortunately also in some present-day churches. I guess for this reason, if for no other, a shirt calling only for people to "sin boldly" rings a bit hollow.

Even if we conclude that Luther had a valid point to make on the subject of faith and works—and I think he did—another point must also be made. Gerhard von Rad taught us that theology, at least sometimes, is not timeless truth, but rather "a particular word relevant to a particular hour in history." In Jeremiah's time other prophets were preaching Isaiah's message of peace, which in Isaiah's time was a true word, but was now a false message. Why? Because God had another word to speak. True words at one time can become false words in another.

Is your life one that reflects the glory of God, one that proceeds from one degree of glory to another? These are questions I believe Christians must ask today, and then answer. You and I must answer them. Reflecting the divine glory is the road to life. Exchanging it for anything inglorious is the road to death.

> God of mercy, God of grace
> Show the brightness of thy face
> Shine upon us, Savior shine
> Fill thy church with light divine
> And thy saving health extend
> Unto earth's remotest end.
> (H. F. Lyte 1793–1847)

AMEN

28

Old Christians but No Old Christianity[1]

Text: 2 Corinthians 4:16

So we do not lose heart. Even though our outer nature is wasting away, our inner nature in being renewed day by day.

It is nearly ten years ago that I first experienced the real impact of this passage. I was having trouble with a right knee that had been injured playing football at North Park Academy. Sitting in my doctor's office in California, the doctor was looking at X-rays of my knee before a surgery that was already scheduled. In my hearing, he exclaimed as pictures came into view on a brightly lighted board, "Advanced arthritis!" Since my first surgery years earlier both sides of the knee bone had deteriorated.

I went over to have a look at the X-rays myself. It was true. They showed a loss of some bone, but I hastened to point out to the good doctor that this bone—like others in my body—was good-sized, and quite a bit still remained. He agreed, expressing the hope that I might get another twenty years out of my knee, but then I might be faced with having to get a knee replacement. I had discovered that my outer nature was beginning to waste away.

Two years later, in New England, I got my first pair of glasses. The doctor in Waterbury, Connecticut, was of a more reassuring nature. He told me I had nothing to worry about. My eyes were simply showing the aging process affecting people between forty and fifty-five. But again, the message was clear: I was getting old.

---

1. Preached at the Covenant Church in Stillman Valley, Illinois, on June 24, 1990.

Old Christians but No Old Christianity

The realization now comes to me more often. Just last Friday, while lunching with senior folks of our church, I lost a piece of tooth on food that should have posed no threat whatever to my teeth—Jell-O salad, potato salad, soft rolls, rice pudding, and Kentucky-fried chicken. I didn't eat the potato chips, which was the only hard food available, and there was no taffy—which has caused trouble in the past—for dessert. My wife decided the Kentucky-fried caused my tooth to break.

In our day, of course, a friendly dentist will have my smile back to what it was before Friday's lunch—and without the pain I remember as a child. And life is wondrously improved with glasses, not to mention eye surgery, which is now becoming routine. My mother will have cataract surgery next month on an outpatient basis! Hip replacements and knee replacements are being done every day, and they are improving. Just this past week I heard about an important advance in knee replacements. Triple bypasses are becoming routine, and liver transplants are being done at the University of Chicago Hospital.

As wonderful as all this is—and it is wonderful—let us not kid ourselves. Our outer natures are wasting away. Sooner or later we must come to terms with aging, even though resistance at times may be strong. We know someone who wears college-style clothes when they are twenty to thirty years out of college. Others of an older age try and keep up with the lingo of high school young people. I chuckle at a middle-aged pastor friend who drives a racy sports car—a statement of sorts showing resistance to the aging process.

There is something to be said for keeping up with the times; nevertheless, we are amused when seeing people attempting to hang on to something that is gone forever. It is just as funny seeing people who resist change—another way of not saying goodbye to yesterday.

How unlike the talk I heard recently during a birthday party for Lillie. Everyone was amazed that this woman could be a smart ninety-five, for she neither looks nor acts her age. Yet in talking with her I was no less amazed at attitudes and reflections untypical of people her age. She knew where she had been; she knew where she was now; and she knew where she was going. Also, she had less concern about a deteriorating vertebrae in her back than I had about my knee.

Linda and I have a good friend in California who retains a marvelous way of affirming the day she is presently living. Every birthday, every year of life, every stage she went through was different and special in its own way.

I've come to greatly admire this. Her outer nature was wasting away, but not her inner nature, which was fresh as almond blossoms in early February.

Which brings us around to what Paul is telling us in our text for the morning. While our outer nature follows a gradual, uneven but nevertheless sure line of descent to deterioration and death, within us ought to be a nature that is daily being renewed.

The ancient Hebrews did not import foreign notions about the rhythms of nature into their religious understanding. Yes, they knew that grass withers and flowers fade, but they cited this only to contrast it with the word of God that stands forever (Isa 40:6–8). Israelites rejected Baal religion and a belief that its god died in winter and came to life again in the spring.

Christian faith, on the other hand, makes far more of renewal and rebirth. Jesus puzzles a Jewish teacher with words about being "born anew." But he himself would later be born anew. For Paul, too, renewal was of great importance. For him the life of faith behaved much like nature, which was constantly being renewed. In our text for the morning Paul says that our inner nature is being renewed every day.

David Nyvall, founder and first president of North Park College, preached a sermon in November 1927 at the fiftieth anniversary of the Covenant Tabernacle Church on Chicago's south side. In it he said:

> Grace remains, but faith is renewed. There are
> old Christians but no old Christianity, in the same
> way as there are old rose bushes but no old roses
> or old fragrance of roses. Old fragrance of roses
> is not fragrance but perfume.[2]

What does he mean? He means that Christians—like all other people—get old. In a hundred ways they can see that they are wearing out, that their strength is on the wane, that their outer nature is wasting away, and one day they will die. But, he says, Christianity—meaning both the individual Christian and the church as a whole—cannot because of its inner nature get old. Its inner nature is being renewed every day. History teaches us that the church is not the church unless it is constantly being renewed. A church that loses its freshness ceases to be the church; its fragrance has been exchanged for perfume.

---

2. Nyvall, *Beacon Lights* (trans. E. Gustav Johnson; Chicago: North Park College Alumni Association, 1933), 17.

Old Christians but No Old Christianity

How then do we accept calls for church renewal? Also, how do we accept calls for individuals within the church to be renewed? Renewal is a sign of God's Spirit at work. Renewal is a sign of our obedience to God; it is rediscovering basic tenets of our faith and finding new ways to live them out. In renewal practices in the church can be called into question, e.g., the way we raise money and for what purpose. Renewal can come when we are open to fresh translations of the Bible and fresh interpretations in preaching. It is a sure sign that our inner nature is being renewed every day when we develop fresh ways of talking about our faith and new ways of living it.

Some today want to hang on to old language in the same way they hang on to old clothes. If they do not hear truths expressed in the same old words, they think the gospel is not being preached, and Jesus Christ is not being lifted up as Savior and Lord. Do we have to ask everyone if they are "saved"? Or do we always have to ask, "Is Christ your Savior?" Do we need to require from everyone a confession that they have been "born again"? So far as we know, Jesus put the "born again" (or "born anew") requirement to only one person, Nicodemus (John 3:3–7). He didn't speak these words to Nathanael (John 1:47). Nathanael was welcomed into the kingdom with different language entirely, and the same was true with others. Jesus met each person on a different level; for some he performed mighty works, which no words could possibly accomplish.

It appears from what John reports about the Nicodemus encounter that the good teacher of Judaism was surprised at Jesus' question; he had never heard such language before. Happily, Billy Graham has now recently come to acknowledge that "born again" is a worn-out term and says perhaps we should quit using it. In the early days of the Mission Covenant Church the commonly asked questions were different ones. People would say, "Är du liver?" ("Are you alive?"), or "Var är det skrivit?" ("Where is it written?") When were you last asked either of these questions?

While it is true that deeds need to transcend whatever language we use, language is nevertheless important. The point to be made about language is that it needs to be fresh, just as trees need new blossoms and rosebushes need new roses. Our witness must radiate life. Which is to say, we need renewal if we are to be fragrant Christians. Paul says it should be happening every day. There is no old Christianity. One cannot carry around the Christianity of Mom or Dad, or anyone else for that matter. Nor can one wear the Christianity of one's youth on the sleeve at twenty, forty, or sixty, any more than one might wear at this age an award earned years ago in school, in Scouts, or in Sunday school. Faith in Christ must each day be something new.

If it is not, we have every reason to "lose heart," for we are getting old. One day, if it has not happened already, we will find that we are old Christians, and the signs will accumulate that our outer nature is wasting away. Even with the new knees and new hips, new glasses and cataract-improved eyes, carpal tunnel surgery and restructured toes, the body is still wearing out.

But Paul says we need not lose heart. God's treasure is within earthen vessels; both death and life are at work within us, and simply need to be put in right perspective. To that end Paul says:

> ... we look not at what can be seen but at what cannot be seen; for what can be seen is temporary, but what cannot be seen is eternal.
> (2 Cor 4:18)

AMEN

29

"Old Soldiers Never Die"[1]

Text: John 8:51

Very truly, I tell you, whoever keeps my word will never see death.

"Old soldiers never die, they just fade away." These words are best remembered as having been spoken by General Douglas MacArthur (1880–1964), American general and commander of the Allied forces in the Pacific during World War II. To a joint meeting of Congress, on April 19, 1951, he said:

> I still remember the refrain of one of the most popular barrack(s) ballads of that day,[2] which proclaimed most proudly that old soldiers never die, they just fade away. I now close my military career and just fade away.

The song appears to have derived from World War I.

After Virginia Ohlson—known to family and friends as Jinny—was made chief of nursing affairs under the Allied Occupation of Japan (SCAP), she became directly responsible to General MacArthur. She had an office in

---

1. Preached at the memorial service for Dr. Virginia M. Ohlson, held at the North Park Covenant Church, Chicago, Illinois, on April 17, 2010. At the time of her death, Virginia was Professor Emerita of the University of Illinois at Chicago. Virginia spent seven years, from 1947 to 1954, in Japan, first under General Douglas MacArthur and the American Occupation where she became Chief of Nursing Affairs of Public Health and Welfare, working with Japanese nurses to reestablish nursing education and practice in Japan. In 1951, when the Occupation was ending, Virginia became Director of Nursing with the Atomic Bomb Casualty Commission in Hiroshima.

2. Written by J. Foley; copyrighted 1920.

the same building as his office, the Dai Ichi Building, across from the moat surrounding the imperial palace in central Tokyo.

MacArthur was characterized by the American president who brought his military career to a close, and even more in a movie made about him some years ago, as an uncommonly headstrong individual. Needless to say, it took such a man to bring the Pacific War to a successful conclusion. There was, however, another side to the man that many Americans do not know. But any surviving Japanese person who remembers him—and not many are still alive—will tell you that he was uncommonly gracious when it came to making the peace.

Jinny told me this many times. MacArthur made it a rule for himself, and all Americans in Japan from 1945 to 1950 under the Occupation, that the Japanese people were not to be shamed, but were to be respected and shown kindness. Jinny said that as a result the Japanese people came to love the man, and that he could walk out of the General Headquarters Building without an escort, with crowds of people gathering just to catch a glimpse of him.

Here Jinny and the good general were of a like mind, and they behaved in a like manner. Jinny loved the Japanese people with a deep love, and her greatest satisfaction in life was to serve them and help heal the wounds of war in any way she could.

Jinny, too, was a soldier. Even before arriving in Japan she received an officer's commission in the army, traveled with soldiers on trains and airplanes going to Japan, and soon after arriving in Tokyo, had a Jeep in which to drive around the city and places more distant.

Now in her last years, she too faded away. At Covenant Home in Chicago she began sleeping more during the day and was doing less and less letter writing. At Northbrook, she got the added care needed at Brandel Skilled Nursing Center. Jinny and my mother had to take separate rooms there, having only afternoon visits when the two of them, who had been close since they were small girls, could talk a bit, sing familiar songs, color pictures, eat popcorn and candy, and play dominoes. It was only in the last few weeks that Jinny was unable to match up the domino numbers correctly. Then the day came when not even these small pleasures were possible. It seemed to be happening again, this time at Covenant Village, Northbrook, that "old soldiers never die, they just fade away."

But we are assembled here today to affirm something greater, for Jinny was a soldier in another army, having lived her life from an early age as a

"Old Soldiers Never Die"

devoted follower of Jesus Christ. She wanted originally to go out as a missionary to China, having been influenced by Ruth Nordlund Nelson of this congregation, who was a public health nurse. Jinny heard Ruth speak about public health nursing at a girls' club meeting at the church when she was thirteen. Then at sixteen, she met Millie Nelson, Covenant missionary to China, who was at the Bible Institute of North Park.

But in 1946 civil war was raging in China, and missionaries were beginning to come home. Some were living across the alley from us in the Missionary Home. By 1949 China was closed to foreign missionaries, and all our Covenant missionaries had relocated to Hong Kong, Formosa (Taiwan), Japan, or returned home. Then an opportunity came for Jinny to go to Japan as a public health nurse under the Occupation. After much prayer and some personal struggle, she decided to go to the nation that only two years earlier had been at war with us. She arrived in Japan in September 1947.

In Japan Jinny was able to carry out missionary work in tandem with her work in nursing, and in this she received the full support of General MacArthur, who hoped that Christianity would take root in Japan. At one point MacArthur wrote a letter to Christian missionaries who had gone home from the Far East asking them to return to Japan to help in the rebuilding of the country.

One of Jinny's great joys during her time in Japan was to be able to organize the Disciple Bible Class among young Japanese nurses. It started with only two nurses, then grew to thirty, and then grew to double that number. Her translator was Mitsuko Saito, later known to many in this church when she came to the States to study. Many young nurses became Christians through this class, but not all. Some remained Buddhists, but they were nevertheless committed to remain as members of the class. I met a couple of these women when I was in Japan in 2008. Jinny also organized a Nurses Christian Fellowship in Japan, another fruit of her missionary work there.

In the Gospel of John, which is where Jinny always began with her Bible Class girls, Jesus is recorded as saying: "Anyone who keeps my word . . . will never see death." It is a mystery, but nevertheless a precious truth, that in Christ one dies and at the same time goes on to live forever. So our final word on this day, which is one not of sorrow but of celebration, is that "another old soldier has not died, but has gone on to join the church triumphant." Thanks be to God. AMEN

Walking with Wisdom

30

Oil Enough to Make the Journey[1]

Advent

Text: Matthew 25:1–12

Then the kingdom of heaven will be like this. Ten bridesmaids took their lamps and went to meet the bridegroom. Five of them were foolish, and five were wise. When the foolish took their lamps, they took no oil with them; but the wise took flasks of oil with their lamps. As the bridegroom was delayed, all of them became drowsy and slept. But at midnight there was a shout, "Look! Here is the bridegroom! Come out to meet him." Then all those bridesmaids got up and trimmed their lamps. The foolish said to the wise, "Give us some of your oil, for our lamps are going out." But the wise replied, "No! there will not be enough for you and for us; you had better go to the dealers and buy some for yourselves." And while they went to buy it, the bridegroom came, and those who were ready went with him into the wedding banquet; and the door was shut. Later the other bridesmaids came also, saying, "Lord, lord, open to us." But he replied, "Truly I tell you, I do not know you."

Sanctify us O Lord in the truth; your word is truth. Amen.

---

1. Preached in the chapel of Union Theological Seminary, Nanjing, China, on November 23, 2007. Translated by Dr. Manhong Lin into Chinese.

Chapters 24 and 25 of Matthew's Gospel contain a discourse by Jesus about his second coming, which is said to have some of the same marks as his first coming: There will be signs on earth and in the heavens—false messiahs, wars and rumors of wars, famines, earthquakes, persecutions, love growing cold, and the sun and moon growing dark. No one, save God, will know the day or the hour. Jesus says not even he knows it (24:36). Great acts of God, as Johannes Weiss once said, are carried out in secret. There will, however, be a delay; and during the delay we are to be in readiness in order that when Jesus does come we may join in the celebration.

The parable of the five wise and five foolish bridesmaids is told to describe and inform us about this hope, reminding us of how we are to live. Matthew is the only Gospel writer to record it. Customs in first-century-AD Palestine were somewhat different from customs today. Marriage celebrations were night affairs. Things began with a procession to the house of the groom, which is where the marriage will take place, although on some occasions weddings are known to have taken place at the bride's house. Today in America, weddings normally—but not always—take place at the bride's church or near the bride's home.

In this particular case the groom and his party will come by the bride's house, or possibly some other location, and pick up the bride and her party, who are waiting there. All will walk together to the house of the groom. Processions of this sort exist today in Afghanistan and in other parts of the world. Since it is night, they need their lamps. There are no streetlights to brighten the way. Even with lamps the bridesmaids had better watch where they are going. I compare it to walking at night in the Congo where I was some years ago. There you very much need to have a flashlight at night.

At the groom's house, before the wedding takes place, there will be a grand dinner. Of great importance here are assumptions we make about when things will begin. There is no set hour or minute as with our weddings. It will happen when it happens. Again I compare it to church services and other festive gatherings in the Congo—people are walking, it may be raining, and one has only a general idea of when things will begin. Everyone knows there could be a delay, and very likely there will be. But when it's time to begin, everyone has to be there.

Here ten bridesmaids are invited to the wedding, waiting, as the parable begins, for the procession to begin. They may be at the bride's home, or at some other location along the way; they are, in any case, waiting to be picked up by the groom and his party, who have been delayed. Five have jars of oil for their lamps; five do not. It is perfectly reasonable that more oil will be needed to complete the journey than what is in each of the bridesmaid's tiny lamps. There is nothing wrong with going to sleep. (Verse 13 with its warning to keep awake is an add-on giving another teaching.) All do it. No need to worry about an alarm clock. Someone will waken them.

Well, the groom comes. The bridesmaids are awakened. Everyone must get up and go, for the groom is there and the bride is ready. Those having their jars of oil prepare to leave. Those who do not make a desperate plea for more oil. Everyone seems to realize that more oil will be needed. And everyone must carry their own lighted lamp, for the procession will move quickly, and one cannot expect to walk in the light of another's lamp. The bridesmaids with the oil jars cannot be faulted for failing to share their oil. They need it. And the other bridesmaids know they need it. However, it seems a twenty-four-hour convenience store is nearby as the five go to a dealer at the last minute to get more oil. And they get it!

However, the wedding procession could not wait. It has gone ahead, and by the time the latecomers arrive the door at the groom's house is barred—which we must understand as an accepted practice in antiquity where there are no porch lights to switch on so one can see who stands outside. The five bridesmaids therefore are not allowed in. Those inside do not know who they are. A voice from inside says: "Truly, I tell you, I do not know you" (v. 12). I am told the same refusal used to obtain years ago in China when you came to the gate of a walled city after dark. You might call to the gatekeeper, but he would not open the gate because he did not know who you were. You could, for all he knows, be a robber. You must then spend the night outside the city, which had its dangers.

So because of a lack of preparation, five young women who were invited to a splendid wedding were unable to join in the celebration. They are treated like those uninvited. They are excluded, not because they were not wanted, for they were wanted. These women, one should note, are neither bad nor immoral; they are simply foolish. They had not enough oil to make the journey.

Jesus in telling this parable gives us a remarkable teaching, saying that foolishness is a companion to faithlessness. People who do not live in readiness for what they know is coming are like people without faith. These people knew the groom was coming, but they acted as if he was not. They knew there could be a delay, but they lived as though there would not be one. They knew waiting time was time for getting ready, but they lived as if waiting time was wasted time.

The parable should be a wake-up call for all of us, for do we not think that exclusion from the kingdom comes largely because of wrongdoing—violating God's laws, living in sin of one sort or another, disbelief or disregard of teachings in the Bible and confirmed by the church? Or is there, perhaps, some overlap between disbelief, disregard, and foolishness? Can foolishness keep people from the heavenly banquet? It seems clearly to be so.

Individual lives and life in the church are seldom better informed. We hardly believe that good times are ahead. We await some procession of excited folk who know where they are going—new leaders, new members perhaps—who will sweep by, pick us up, and take us with them. I have heard people say, "When something begins to happen, then you'll see me there." These are the people who, when things do begin to happen, beg to travel on someone else's oil. Why? Because they have none of their own; they are running on empty.

There are always times when we feel as if we are living in a sort of waiting period, when not much of anything is happening. I'm talking about quiet times, unexciting times, times that are dull, even boring. It is easy to get depressed during such times. Which is all the more reason why we have to be careful. Not only is it possible to waste valuable time while we are waiting, but more important, our idleness—worse yet, our recklessness—may disqualify us from good times ahead.

In the Christian life we need to be reminded of the great promises of God, that good times are being planned right now for each one of us and for the church worldwide. Signs will be given, which some among the faithful will see. These are meant not to prove, but to awaken. God plans his great works in secret so no one knows precisely when they will occur. As before, there will be delays. But during the waiting time we must be in active readiness, so when the celebration takes place we can join in. Some, simply because of foolishness, will be left out. I leave you then with the question: "Have you oil enough to make the journey?" AMEN

31

The Limits of Wisdom[1]

Text: Luke 4:21–30

Then he began to say to them, "Today this scripture has been fulfilled in your hearing." All spoke well of him and were amazed at the gracious words that came from his mouth. They said, "Is not this Joseph's son?" He said to them, "Doubtless you will quote to me this proverb, 'Doctor, cure yourself!' And you will say, 'Do here also in your hometown the things that we have heard you did at Capernaum.'" And he said, "Truly I tell you, no prophet is accepted in the prophet's hometown. But the truth is, there were many widows in Israel in the time of Elijah, when the heaven was shut up three years and six months, and there was a severe famine over all the land; yet Elijah was sent to none of them except to a widow at Zarephath in Sidon. There were also many lepers in Israel in the time of the prophet Elisha, and none of them was cleansed except Naaman the Syrian." When they heard this, all in the synagogue were filled with rage. They got up, drove him out of the town, and led him to the brow of a hill on which their town was built, so that they might hurl him off the cliff. But he passed through the midst of them and went on his way.

There is a renewed interest today in wisdom. Sunday school classes and Bible study groups are looking at the wisdom books of the Bible, i.e., Job, Proverbs, Ecclesiastes, the Song of Solomon, and Psalms. In society at large is a fascination with the wisdom of other cultures. Browsing through the

---

1. Preached at the Covenant Church in Hilmar, California, on October 22, 1978.

bookstore you will find books on African proverbs and the traditional wisdom of China and Japan.

This may result from the fact that we have more leisure, affording us the luxury of being more reflective. In antiquity wisdom flourished in the upper class—amidst people such as King Solomon, and Job, who was a man of wealth. Yet busy people in all levels of society are reflective enough to have a few proverbs ready to quote.

Our current interest in wisdom may be a response to the explosion of knowledge that has hit the modern world. New explanations challenge the old. New ways of doing things challenge the old. All of these force us to be reflective and to seek wisdom. Twenty-five years ago when I was living in the farm country of Iowa the wisdom of using chemical fertilizer was being debated. Today its wisdom is again being debated, although with different results. We are also wondering about the wisdom of putting preservatives in foods, about MacDonald's using tons of Styrofoam, and so forth.

Morals and ethics are favorite wisdom topics, and in the wake of Vietnam and Watergate we are debating the extent to which moral and ethical principles should inform politics, business, and the military. Do police have the right to break into apartments to get information on drugs? What exactly constitutes sexual harassment? Must a candidate for the presidency reveal explicit sexual behavior or misbehavior?

Add to all this questions Christians are asking about the will of God. What is God doing in the changing world of today, and what he is doing amidst the myriad of complexities in our lives? Faith is not simple. Christian faith is and should be a questioning faith, one that weighs options and admits doubt. People who question and admit doubt are people who seek wisdom about what they themselves are doing, the wisdom of what others are doing, and the wisdom of what God is doing.

What is wisdom? We can begin by stating the obvious: Most everyone will agree that wisdom is not the same thing as knowledge; it is greater than knowledge, which is to say that while a wise person may have knowledge, not every person possessing knowledge is wise. Francis Bacon, advisor to Queen Elizabeth, was called by some "the most learned fool in the world."

Having said this, it nevertheless remains true that you cannot be a wise person without knowledge. There are people who may disagree with this, who think they can be wise even though they don't know anything, but they are mistaken. To be wise you must possess knowledge—knowledge gained from books, from a teacher, from practical experience, from Mother

The Limits of Wisdom

or Dad, or from someone older and more experienced than you. You can also gain knowledge from people younger than yourself—indeed from small children. We learn some things by ourself, some things by accident, some things by mistake, and some things because God reveals them to us. But the point is one cannot be wise if one does not possess knowledge.

Yet if we possess knowledge, even in great quantity, that is not to say we are wise. Wisdom has at least two other characteristics. A wise person is able to discriminate amongst the knowledge he or she possesses. A wise person knows that certain things are good and certain things are bad. A wise person can tell whether nice words are a genuine expression of graciousness or "so much butter and cream." A wise person reads some books but leaves others alone. A wise person does not drink in everything even from a favorite author; he or she will sort it out, accepting some things and rejecting others. A wise person listens to some music and leaves other music alone. A wise person does not believe everything teachers, preachers, and even great evangelists tell them. God's Word does not come in pure form; it comes in some wonderful way from the fumbling efforts of all of us called to preach, teach, and bear witness to Jesus Christ. Solomon was a wise man because he was able to discern the real mother of the baby placed before him (1 Kgs 3:16–28).

Thirdly, a wise person is one who makes practical use of his or her knowledge. It is not enough just to know something, even to inwardly discern the truth. You must tell others what you know and what you have sorted out; you must act on the knowledge and discernment you possess. The wise person is a teller and a doer. Jesus said, "Everyone then who hears these words of mine and acts on them will be like a wise man who built his house on rock" (Matt 7:24).

In ancient times the wise man was a counselor to the king—a kind of secretary of state. He advised the best course of action to take in war, advising also on how to make peace. Fathers passed on wisdom to their sons, warning them of hidden dangers, telling how to succeed in life, expounding the virtues of a good wife, and so forth. Mothers passed on wisdom to their daughters. Read the book of Proverbs. To be a wise person, then, you must act upon your knowledge or whatever discernment you have gained over time.

The most popular wisdom in antiquity was the proverb. The same is true today. Almost everyone has proverbs they quote from time to time.

Some people continually quote proverbs, often the same ones. I remember the proverbs I heard most often as a boy:

Haste makes waste (my mother)

If the shoe fits, put it on (my high school science teacher)

Here lies John Day; he had the right of way (my grandpa)

A cobbler's son has no shoes (China missionary)

Never let the sun go down on your wrath (my grandmother; cf. Eph 4:26)

I used to tell my kids, "There are some mistakes you can't make even once."

 Each of these is a little gem of wisdom containing a proven insight about life: an insight culled from collective experience; an insight useful in discriminating right from wrong, good from bad, true from false; an insight one could pass on to others—children usually—to help them succeed and avoid harm.

 Jesus, in our text for today, begins his teaching following a Scripture reading by placing a proverb into the mouths of the assembled folk at Nazareth: "Doctor, cure yourself." The proverb was well-known, as we know from both Greek and Jewish sources. The Greek poet Euripides (485–406 BC) derided one who was the "doctor of others, yet running (himself) with sores," a proverb still being quoted nine hundred years later. In the Jewish Talmud a rabbi is quoted as saying, "Doctor, heal your own limp" (*Bereshith Rabba*, 23). All these proverbs point up the incongruity of a sick doctor, one who perhaps does not take the prescriptions he gives to others. There is a similar incongruity in the cobbler's son who has no shoes, or the minister's son or daughter who behaves more shamefully than other sons and daughters.

 From the New Testament are other parallels. In the Sermon on the Mount Jesus talks about getting the log out of your own eye before trying to remove the speck from your neighbor's eye (Matt 7:5). People at the foot of the cross mock Jesus, saying, "He saved others; let him save himself if he is the Messiah of God" (Luke 23:35). And Paul, speaking to his fellow Jew says, "You, then, that teach others, will you not teach yourself?" (Rom 2:21).

 Here in our text the proverb is given a somewhat broader meaning, as we can see from the statement that accompanies it: "Do here also in your hometown the things that we have heard you did at Capernaum" (v. 23).

The Limits of Wisdom

The point is not that Jesus himself needs healing, but that the home folks in Nazareth do. These people want to see miracles in their own town, telling Jesus in effect, "Charity begins at home."

Jesus, however, counters with another proverb that may also have been well-known: "No prophet is accepted in the prophet's hometown" (cf. John 4:44). This proverb is 180 degrees from the first one. Jesus cannot perform miracles among his own. People are reminded of the time of Elijah and Elisha if they want to know why. They get the message, and becoming enraged they nearly succeed in pushing him off a cliff outside the village.

The lesson to be learned here is that proverbs, while they give genuine insight into life and can be used over and over again, still have but limited usefulness. They are not universal truths applying to all people in all times. Both of the proverbs cited by Jesus were true, yet only one was true in this particular situation.

So it is with the proverbs we use. My mother was a fast-moving sort of person who admired this same quality in others. She would say approvingly of someone, "He doesn't let any grass grow under his feet." She could also have said, "The early bird catches the worm." Both underscore the wisdom of fast action, sometimes used to prod people to get going. Yet mother's proverbs depended on the situation. If I went too fast, tripped, and fell, she would say, "Well, haste makes waste." Strangely enough, my mother married a man who could not hurry if he had to. My dad was level-headed and sure-footed, but seldom early enough to catch the worm; grass literally grew under his feet. So what did my mother say about him? "Still water runs deep"!

A young girl ponders whether some time away from her boyfriend will not do the two of them good. One friend tells her it is a good idea: "Absence makes the heart grow fonder." But from another friend she gets this advice: "When the cat's away, the mice will play." Uncle Pete agrees. He says, "Out of sight, out of mind." What should she do?

The limits of wisdom were noticed by the compiler of Proverbs. In chapter 26 are two proverbs right next to each other giving precisely opposite advice. The first in v. 4 says:

> Do not answer fools according to their folly
> or you will be a fool yourself

This counsels the wise person to keep still when a fool taunts him. To answer such a person is to play the same game and make a fool of yourself. But the proverb in v. 5 says:

> Answer fools according to their folly
> or they will be wise in their own eyes.

Here the wise person is counselled not to be silent when taunted by a fool. Better to retort in kind, the proverb says, lest the fool go away thinking he is wise.

Wisdom—even the most perceptive wisdom—has its limits. The book of Job presents two types of wisdom—the traditional wisdom expressed by Job's friends, which is that sickness and suffering must be the result of one's sin, and another wisdom expressed by Job, that evil people—many of them—remain alive and well while he though innocent suffers to the point of death.

Job prepares us for the New Testament gospel, which one cannot comprehend without realizing that God, by sending Jesus to the cross, stood traditional Jewish wisdom on its head. This was a wisdom that said salvation is in life—Abraham's son Isaac, Joseph, the exodus, Jeremiah, the remnant in exile, and so forth. But John 3:16 says that God gave his son over to death in order that the world might be saved!

Jewish teachers could quote Deuteronomy, where it says that anyone hanged on a tree is cursed by God (Deut 21:23). But Paul did not believe Jesus was cursed by God. He tells the Galatians: "Christ redeemed us from the curse of the law by becoming a curse for us" (Gal 3:13). And he tells the Corinthians that God has made foolish the wisdom of the world (1 Cor 1:20). Paul is not talking here about all wisdom, but traditional wisdom that puts a curse on Jesus because he was hung on a cross. It is "Christ crucified," a stumbling block to Jews demanding signs, and Greeks seeking wisdom.

This morning as we approach the Lord's table may we know that the way to God is not ultimately through wisdom, important as wisdom is, but through faith in the person of Jesus. Wisdom only brings us to the brink, from which we must take that grand leap called faith. AMEN

32

"A Time to Be Born and a Time to Die"[1]

New Year's

Text: Ecclesiastes 3:1–2a

For everything there is a season, and a time for every matter under heaven: a time to be born, and a time to die.

The Christmas story centered on a baby, placing the accent squarely on birth and life. But as we read Luke's Gospel we find that following the story—separated only by the brief note about Jesus being circumcised and given his name when he was eight days old—is another report almost certainly intended to counterbalance the message of Jesus' birth. It is a report about two people who have reached the end of life and will soon pass from the scene. It accents old age, even death.

That Luke should juxtapose young and old in his Christmas story should not surprise us, for frequently we do much the same thing in our own Christmas celebrations. I'm thinking of the new baby in our midst who is given an inordinate amount of attention, or the young children—perhaps the very youngest—chosen to pass out gifts under the tree. Do we not also focus our attention on the children as they open their gifts? And we honor

1. Preached at the Covenant Church in Menominee, Michigan, on December 27, 1992.

the old in our families, asking grandpa perhaps to read the Christmas story or offer the prayer when we are sitting around the table. We might even want Grandma or Grandpa to hold the newborn so we can take a picture of them together.

New Year's, too, celebrates the arrival of the new and departure of the old. The *Chicago Tribune* used to have a front-page cartoon every New Year's Day of a baby arriving with a tag of the new year and a bearded old man with the tag of the old year on his way out.

In our New Testament lesson of Luke 2:25-38 the baby Jesus is about six weeks old. His parents have brought him to the temple where they will offer the sacrifice for the firstborn son (Exod 13:1-16), also another sacrifice for Mary's purification (Lev 12). According to Jewish law, forty days (roughly six weeks) had to pass before the mother would be judged fully cleansed and healed from her delivery. Up until a century ago the custom in Sweden was for the mother to be brought to church one month after her child was born and be presented, as it were, to the congregation. This custom was rooted in the biblical law of Leviticus 12.

Some years ago my son David and I were invited guests at a coming-out party for a new mother in the African village of Gbado, Zaire (Congo). This was a similar type of celebration to which the whole village was invited. The mother, who had not been seen since her baby was born, came out of the house near to where we were assembled, with baby in arms, preceded by her mother, and was seated next to her husband in the midst of villagers and guests for a not-too-brief ceremony. My David, who was the youngest guest, was given the seat next to the chief of the village, who besides being the most honored was also the oldest man present. When Mary and Joseph and the baby Jesus were at the temple, two elderly people were among the group assembled. One was a man named Simeon, the other a woman named Anna.

Simeon, we are told, was righteous and devout, someone "looking for the consolation of Israel." He was waiting for the messianic age to dawn. Moreover, the Holy Spirit had told him that he would not see death before he beheld the Messiah. The picture of old Simeon with babe in arms speaks for itself. His words of thanksgiving are intermixed with benediction:

> Master, now you are dismissing your servant in peace
>   according to your word
> for my eyes have seen your salvation
>   which you have prepared in the presence of all peoples

"A Time to Be Born and a Time to Die"

> a light for revelation to the Gentiles
> and for glory to your people Israel
>
> (Luke 2:29–32)

There is a time to be born, says Simeon, and a time to die. But in this old man there is more affirmation and less resignation; Simeon's words are a long way from those from the one reputed to have written Ecclesiastes. I sense some real joy in Simeon's words (cf. v. 27). Simeon has been living in expectation, and now the time of his expectation has come. His expectation is twofold: (a) Simeon knows the promise made to Israel long ago that God would send a messianic king, and (b) Simeon held dear a personal word from the Lord that the awaited event would occur during his lifetime.

The first expectation he shares with all Israel. We know even more today, in light of the Dead Sea Scrolls discovered over forty years ago, that expectations ran high among the Jews about the coming of their messiah. The second expectation gives meaning to his own life. For perhaps many years this man had lived with a personal hope that he would actually live to see the day dawn.

And then there is Anna. She is often eclipsed by Simeon, and that is unfortunate because she very much belongs to the story. Luke among the New Testament writers gives more attention to women who figure into the gospel drama, and it is no accident that he includes in his report of the temple ceremony participation by both an older man and an older woman. The eclipse of Anna may well be due to subsequent liturgy, where the Nunc Dimittis (Song of Simeon) has been paired with the Magnificat (Song of Mary) found in Luke 1:46–55.

Anna is a prophetess, one of a very few in Israel. Luke gives us a few details of her life, but only for one purpose, viz., to emphasize how long and how faithfully she has awaited this day. Anna had a husband for seven short years; she is now eighty-four, which means she was a widow for fifty, perhaps sixty years. That is a long time. This woman was living when Pompey and the Romans came to occupy Syria and Palestine ending centuries of Greek rule; she lived during the reign of Julius Caesar (46–44 BC); she lived throughout the long reign of Herod the Great. All these years, we are told, she went regularly to the temple, day and night, to fast and pray! Now she rejoices along with Simeon that God has fulfilled his long-standing promise to Israel. After seeing the baby Jesus she gives thanks to God and tells the good news to others present.

No doubt there was also a sense in which her own personal life was fulfilled. She was a prophetess, so she knew full well what it meant when prophetic words had come to pass. Her patient wait all these years was now a witness that God's word does not return void, nor do the faithful hope in vain.

Can you imagine what her life must have been all these years? We don't know, of course, but very likely her biography might not have made particularly interesting reading. Yet so far as Luke is concerned, her life is important because after days and days—indeed years and years—of praying and fasting she now sees the promises of God fulfilled. This one hour puts all those earlier years in perspective. She had a hope, something to look forward to, and that made her days worth living. Because of this hope she is now, at eighty-four years of age, able to speak words of joy instead of lying around moping about how cruel life had been since her husband died. She found there was a time to be born and a time to die. According to the biblical view, time is not on a wheel; it has a beginning and an end. So also must we keep in mind that life too has a beginning and end.

This story lifts up another important dimension of the Hebrew and Christian view of time. With God is movement from promise to fulfillment. Anna and Simeon both symbolize an Israel awaiting fulfillment of God's promises. And they symbolize the later church that likewise awaits the fulfillment of God's promise to send Jesus back when the scroll of human history is rolled up.

Living with anticipation gives spirit and zest. People who have anticipations for the future are people who remain uncrushed by the past; people who have the wherewithal to rise above troves of sentimental memories; people who are as prepared to die as they were to live. I remember my grandmother telling me that "anticipation is greater than the real thing." I never agreed with her, and still don't, but I have come to realize the truth she was trying to get across. I know that when you have an exciting event out ahead, your outlook of the present is altered.

I remember as a young boy of about sixteen, the age when one is caught up in the excitement of impending dates with young girls, that I discovered when I had an exciting date to look forward to, my Saturday work was done with ease and joy; the grass was nothing to cut; the car was fun to wash; the snow could be shoveled with ease; errands were run without effort. This is still the case when I look forward to fun things with

"A Time to Be Born and a Time to Die"

my wife and children. Exciting hopes give strength and vigor to surmount problems of the present.

In recent years we have seen how hopes of entire nations have been kept alive when they should have been crushed by bad government and oppressive political systems. People are now crying for joy because the day of their consolation has come. Solidarity is recognized and has brought into power in a new Republic of Poland; Hungary has rewritten its constitution and proclaimed itself no longer a communist nation; the Berlin Wall has come down; Czechoslovakia has renounced the Russian invasion of 1967, revised its constitution, and formed a government led by someone who not long ago was in jail. This past week a Christmas tree stood in the square of Prague; people in Bulgaria are now able to celebrate Christmas in churches, and in Romania carols are being sung by children, and rations on bread have ended. In Romania people were ready to die because they were also ready to live.

We who are Christians are called by God to press forward with anticipation to those things that lie ahead. Paul says since he has made Christ his own, he forgets what lies behind and strains forward to what lies ahead (Phil 3:13). We have a promise the whole church shares—that this One who came as a baby will return one day in power to bring us unto himself. And we have, or should have, individual promises that God has given each one of us. Whatever they are, may we live in the hope that one day they will come to pass. And may our New Year's not be just a time to sing about old acquaintances, as good as these are. May it be a time to live in anticipation of great promises from God—for the 1990s and beyond! AMEN

Name Index

Almquist, Arden, 41
Amerson, Philip A, vii, ix
Anderson, Richard, 41
Anselm, Saint, 61, 62
Aquinas, Saint Thomas, 61

Bacon, Francis, 162
Bonhoeffer, Dietrich, 15, 85
Brooke, George J, xiv note
Bunyan, John, xiv

Calvin, John, 45, 46
Constantine I, Emperor 26
Cox, Harvey, 33

Edwards, K. Morgan, vii, viii, ix
Elizabeth I, Queen, 162
Engelbert, Ernst, 44
Erikson, Erik, 117, 118, 119, 120, 123, 129, 134, 135, 136, 138

Foss, Claude W. xv note

Gamaliel I, Rabbi, 133
Gordon, General Charles, 26
Graham, Billy, 149

Hallberg, Anna, 33
Hillel the Elder, 133
Hitler, Adolf, 63
Holmgren, Fred, 17
Hultman, J. A., 14

Jerome, Saint, 142
Johnson, E. Gustav, 148 note

Johnson, Obed, xv note

Kelly, Thomas, 92
Kierkegaard, Søren, 83
Koehn, Lois, 37

Larson, Norman, 33
Lenin, Nikolai, 25
Levinson, Daniel, 123 124, 125
Liland, Guro, 61
Liland, Peder, 61
Lin, Manhong, 157 note
Lombard Ruth, 33
Lund, Nils, 14
Lundbom, David, 61, 168
Lundbom, Jack R. xiv, note
Lundbom, Joan, 33
Lundbom, Linda, 37, 45, 51, 52, 147
Luther, Martin, 4, 27, 45, 97, 117, 133, 143, 144
Lyte, H. F., 145

MacArthur, General Douglas, 151, 152, 153
Matson, Edla, 130
Matson, Peter, 14
Melanchthon, Philip 143
Michelangelo, 142
Milton, John, 124
Morowitz, Harold J., 104, 105
Muilenburg, James, xiii, 17, 18

Nagurski, Bronco, 14
Nelson, Mildred, 153
Nelson, Ruth Nordlund, 153

Name Index

Nyvall, David, 14, 148

Ohlson, Otto, 50, 51
Ohlson, Virginia M., 151, 152
Ohlson, Winfrid, 51
Ohlson, Winnie, 51
Olsson, Karl, 14
Ottander, O. A., xv

Pius XII, Pope, 32
Pritchard, James A., 93 note

Rad, Gerhard von, 144
Ricoeur, Paul, 6
Robinson, John A. T., 33
Rogers, Will, 91
Rutström, Anders Carl, xv

Saito, Mitsuko, 153
Sallman, Warner, 14
Sheehy, Gail, 123
Speakman, Frederick, 88
Stein, Gertrude, 4

Thornbloom, Robert, 41
Tillich, Paul, 33
Tournier, Paul, 49, 50, 51, 53

Way, Arthur S. 136 note
Weborg, John, 106
Wesley, John, xiv, xv note
Westburg, Sigurd, 41
Wickstrom, Marvin, 9, 41 note
Wynette, Tammy, 52

Zedong, Mao, 26

Scripture Index

with supplement on Old Testament Pseudepigrapha and Rabbinic Writings

OLD TESTAMENT

Genesis

3:8	31
4:23–24	47
5:24	32
8:20–21	83
12	58
22	83
28:10–17	31
28:15	8
43:14	4
50:20	126

Exodus

3	3, 5, 7
3:11–14	3
3:12	6, 8
3:14	6
3:15	3n
4:22	47
13:1–16	168
16:23	4
20:2	47
22:26–27	112
23:4–5	89–90
32:34	6
33	6, 7
33:18	142
33:19–20	6
33:19	11
34	141
34:6	79
34:29–35	140
34:29	141

Leviticus

12	168
19:18	89

Deuteronomy

4:36	31
4:39	31
5:33	xiii
6:4	16
6:5	89
6:7	xiii
7:6	72
8:6	xiii
9:14	107
10:12–11:1	89
10:12	xiii
11:19	xiii
11:22	xiii
14:1–2	83
14:28–29	72
16:9–15	72
21:23	166

Scripture Index

Deuteronomy (continued)

22:1–4	90
23:9–14	31
24:17	112
26:12–13	72
26:15	31
27:19	112
30:11–14	42, 47
30:15–20	xiii
32:22	80
33:2	141
34:6	26
34:10–12	14

Joshua

1:5	8
24	xiii, 57

Judges

6:16	8
16:25	84

1 Samuel

2:12–17	84
2:29	84
3:14	84
4:18	84
10:22	120
13	83
14:36–45	121
15:17	120
15:22–23	121
15:22	43, 82
16:14	121
31	121

2 Samuel

11:1	131
13	131
15:19–22	53
15:20	4
16:7–8	57
19:16–23	57

1 Kings

1–2	132
1:15–31	130
3:16–28	163
17	101
18:28	83

2 Kings

2:9–12	14
2:11	32
4:1	112
9:22	97

Esther

4:16	4

Job

2:9	93
2:13	93
24:3	112
24:9	112
31:35	92
38:1—41:34	92
42	137
42:3	62, 92, 93
42:6	93
42:7–8	93

Psalms

1	xiv
4:4	78
22	122
30:5	80
37:8	80
37:11	24
103:9	80
106:19–20	144
126:5–6	99
126:5	99
128	69–70
128:3–4	69
132:13–18	21
132:13–14	31
139:7–12	30–31

Scripture Index

Proverbs

2	xiv
14:29	79
15:18	79
16:32	79, 80
19:11	79
26:4	165
26:5	166
29:20	93

Ecclesiastes

3:1–2a	167
7:9	79

Isaiah

5:2	71
5:7	71
40–55	126
40:6–8	148
41:10	8
43:5	8
55:6–7	113

Jeremiah

1–20	137
1:4–12	58
1:5	111, 137
1:8	8
1:14–19	22
1:19	8
2:11	144
2:13	111
2:21	71
3:12	81
5:28	112
6:13–15	96
6:14	97
6:16	xiv
6:21	xiv
7:1–15	23
7:8–11	30
11:18–23	23
15:16–17	58, 97
15:18	58, 111
15:20	8
19:1–20:6	23
20:14–18	111
20:18	137
21:8–10	xiii–xiv
23:23–24	30
25:31	7
26	23
26:12	137
26:18	23
26:24	23, 137
30–31	126
31:31–34	109
32:6–12	126
32:36–44	126
36:26	23
36:48	23
37:11–16	24
37:17–21	24
38:2	xiv
38:6	24
38:17–18	xiv
39:15–18	111
40:1–6	19
40:4	24
42:7–22	xiv
45	111
50:31–32	7
50:38	7
51:47	7
51:52	7

Ezekiel

3:3	59
3:14–15	59
3:15	93
11:22–23	32
16:1–7	72

Hosea

8:7	101

Amos

1:3–2:3	7
5:21–24	86
6:4–6	86
9:1–4	31
9:5–6	31

Scripture Index

Micah

7:18	81

Habakkuk

3:3-4	141

Malachi

4:5-6	14, 32, 142

NEW TESTAMENT

Matthew

1:23	8, 32
5:5	24
5:16	144
5:21-22	77
5:22-26	86
7:5	164
7:7	113
7:13-14	xiv
7:15-20	xvn
7:24-27	41, 47
7:24	163
8:11	32
10:34	98
11:28-30	43, 44
17:9	143
17:10-13	142
20:1-16	7, 12
21:15-16	134
23:37	24
24-25	158
24:36	158
25:1-12	157
25:12	159
25:13	159
25:14-30	11, 128-129
25:31-46	90
28:20	8, 32

Mark

9:9	143
9:24	62
9:30-32	61
14:53-62	94
16:8	27
16:19	32
16:23	27

Luke

1:46-55	169
2:25-38	168
2:27	169
2:29-32	168-169
4:21-30	161
4:23	164
6:21b	101
6:25b	101
9	15
9:21	143
9:28-36	13
9:35	15
9:46-48	17
10:25-28	90
10:30-37	72
13:28	32
15:3-7	87
15:29-30	9
16:19-31	32
17:20	110
17:21	110
17:22	110
17:26	110
17:28	111
17:34-36	112
18-20	15
18:1-8	109
18:8	110, 113
19:1-10	87
23:35	164
24:28-35	25
24:50-51	32

John

1:1-14	66
1:47	149

Scripture Index

3:1–21	141
3:3–7	149
3:13	32
3:14–16	63
3:16	35, 38, 46, 114, 166
4:1–42	72, 87
4:44	165
6:67	121
8:1–11	87
8:51	151
11	138
11:33	94
11:35	94
11:37	94
12:24	100
13:34	89
14	53
14:1–6	49
14:2	53
14:5	53
15:13	90
19:22	5
19:26–27	117
20	27
20:17	32
21:18	56
21:19	56
21:20–22	55
21:21	56
21:22	56

Acts

1:9–11	32
4:12	13
5:34–39	133
9:26–27	106
9:31	106
15	17, 106
16:3	17
22:3	133
23:5	94

Romans

1:22–23	144
1:24–26	144
2:21	164
3:23	143
5:2	143
5:8	87
6:4	123
11:18	23
12:21	63

1 Corinthians

1:20	166
6:19–20	48
6:20	144
10:31	144
11:27–32	86
13	87
13:12	33
15:36	100

2 Corinthians

3:4–18	141
3:18	140, 143
4:16	146
4:18	150
5:17	143
9:15	38

Galatians

1:17	106
3:13	166
5:1–14	46
5:7	xiv

Ephesians

4:22–24	143
4:26	78, 81
6:4	78

Philippians

3:13	171

Colossians

1:27	144
3:21	78

2 Timothy

4:7–8	xiv

SCRIPTURE INDEX

Hebrews

13:8	68

James

1:19	79

Revelation

1:4	68
3:15–17	65
3:18–19	67
3:22	57
7:9–10	139
7:12	139

∽

OLD TESTAMENT PSEUDEPIGRAPHA

4 Ezra

7:3–15	xiv

Slavonic Enoch

30:15	xiv

Testament of Abraham

11	xiv

Testament of Asher

1:3–9	xiv

∽

RABBINIC WRITINGS

Bereshith Rabba

23	164